Zebras & Cheetahs

Zebras & Cheetahs

Look Different and Stay Agile to Survive the Business Jungle

Micheal J. Burt and Colby B. Jubenville

WILEY

Published by John Wiley & Sons, Inc., Hoboken, New Jersey.
Published simultaneously in Canada.

For general information about our other products and services, please contact our Customer Care Department within the United States at (800) 762-2974, outside the United States at (317) 572-3993 or fax (317) 572-4002.

Wiley publishes in a variety of print and electronic formats and by print-on-demand. Some material included with standard print versions of this book may not be included in e-books or in print-on-demand. If this book refers to media such as a CD or DVD that is not included in the version you purchased, you may download this material at http://booksupport.wiley.com. For more information about Wiley products, visit www.wiley.com.

Library of Congress Cataloging-in-Publication Data:

Burt, Micheal J.
    Zebras and cheetahs : look different and stay agile to survive the business jungle/ Micheal J. Burt and Colby B. Jubenville.
        pages cm
    ISBN 978-1-118-63180-5 (cloth); ISBN 978-1-118-64478-2 (ebk); ISBN 978-1-118-64477-5 (ebk); ISBN 978-1-118-64470-6 (ebk)
    1. Organizational change.   2. Organizational effectiveness.   3. Organizational behavior.
4. Leadership. I. Jubenville, Colby B., 1971–II. Title.
    HD58.8.B8836 2013
    658.4'09—dc23

                                                                                          2013001368

Printed in the United States of America

10 9 8 7 6 5 4 3 2 1

From Micheal
To my new beautiful daughter, Ella Grace. Here's hoping that one day you become the Zebras and Cheetahs Leader we discuss in the book and beat to your own drum, stand out versus fit in, and get better versus merely getting along.

From Colby
To my parents, who taught me to look different, my children, who help me run faster, and my wife, who challenges me to be agile.

Contents

Foreword

Most forewords tell you about the book you're about to read. I'd rather you just read it for yourself.

Let me tell you a little about why you should be interested in what Micheal and Colby have to say in this book.

Everybody needs a coach. Whether you're trying to lose weight or build a business, a coach can make all the difference in the world, all the difference between success and failure. Micheal is a coach in the best sense of the word. He challenges, he encourages, he provokes, he supports, he calls you on your "stuff," he helps you discover strengths that you didn't even know you had.

Colby is a strategist. Colby helps answer the tough question. First let's identify the easy question: The easy question is "What should I do?" I think that on some level, almost everybody knows what to do. The tough question is "How do I do it?" That's strategy, and without a sound strategy the knowledge of what to do is useless.

The combination of a great coach and a great strategist creates a unique perspective for understanding and a powerful force for action.

The metaphors of Zebras and Cheetahs, the Concrete Jungle, the 10,000-pound Gorilla, and more that are used in this book make perfect sense. Micheal and Colby have taken concepts like dominant aspiration and made them useful, and that's the difference between this book and so many others about success in life, career, and business.

There's great skill involved in making challenging ideas simple and understandable. Whether in their speaking, their consultative work with clients, on their radio show, or in this book, Micheal and Colby demonstrate that skill in spades, and the beneficiary (in the case of this book) is you. If you're like me, you'll find yourself nodding your head in agreement and recognition as you read this book. You'll have that sense of "Hey, that's exactly what I'm going through" throughout the text.

But the true payoff isn't just that Micheal and Colby feel your pain—it's that they've got the cure. It's not silver bullets. It's not secrets of success. It's in ways of looking at, thinking about, and taking action on your challenges and opportunities that make absolute sense. The real payoff is when you find yourself thinking "Hey! I can do this stuff!" It's the inspiration and the how-to's that move you to take action that can change your career and your life.

I read a lot of books. Heck, I've even written a few myself. My hope is that the books I write have the kind of meaningful, positive impact on people that this book has had on me, and that I'm confident it will have on you.

Welcome to the jungle.

Joe Calloway, author of *Becoming a Category of One—How Extraordinary Companies Transcend Commodity and Defy Comparison* and *Be the Best at what Matters Most: The Only Strategy You Will Ever Need*

Preface

I'm 30,000 feet in the air on a flight to Charlotte, North Carolina, to work with one of the top 50 builders in the United States—the second of the top 100 that my firm has landed in the past two years. I always carry a good book with me wherever I travel; for this trip, I've decided to reread Tim Ferris's famed *The 4-Hour Workweek* for the fifth time. I think the concept of *Lifestyle Design* is about to sink in as his book has forced me to not only look at the drivers of the business Models I evaluate but also the actual vehicles people use to advance their strategy. I'm starting to understand that sometimes it's not the vehicle's driver that poses the major problem in getting from point A to point B; rather it's the *actual vehicle* the 'driver is using to get there. It's important to look at both the strategy and the people as they relate to growth, and many times it takes a fresh perspective and someone who specializes in finding and filling the missing structures companies have to take complicated growth and make it simple and engaging.

I've been working as a coach and thought Leader to small entrepreneurial firms and multibillion-dollar companies over the past several years. During this time, I've witnessed a constant problem that keeps people from breaking through their own ceilings of success—a problem that stems from two places: their Model (or lack of one) and their people. Even if they do have the right Model, there's often a substantial gap between what their people know they're *supposed* to do and what they *actually* do. People nowadays seem to be more confused than ever; they're living in chaotic environments with little or no direction on how to achieve growth. In short, they don't know where to go or what to do. This is the infamous and oft-cited "execution gap." And it's also the reason they need someone who specializes in activating their potential.

Every single one of us has likely heard at one point or another that we've got more potential in the tank. But since no one really knows how to squeeze it out of their people in a systematic and coordinated way, growth tends to be random and sporadic, resulting in false starts, good intentions, and mediocre results.

That's where I come in. I know how to get the potential out of the people—and it begins with taking complicated growth and then making it simple and easy to understand. It also has to do with focusing the group's energy on some dominant aspiration, and building something people can emotionally sink their teeth into and get involved in. This is where the *Zebras and Cheetahs Model* comes into play.

Over the years, I've found that many of the Models that organizations are currently using simply don't work. As a former championship coach turned entrepreneur and business builder, I've developed a system that has served multiple disciplines in athletics, financial services, real estate, insurance, and even prison rehabilitation, producing growth of up to 45 percent in a one-year cycle by adding the Model we write about in this book and a coach who engages people in a set of consistent and systematic behaviors that allows them to do something tomorrow they simply cannot do today. Many of the Models I've seen in companies simply aren't sufficient to become the vehicle that drives new performance; and sometimes organizations just have the wrong players on the team to execute the Model. This is why I begin work with *any* company that wants me to drive a dominant focus by asking them to answer three questions before we dive in:

1. **Do we have the right players on this team?** No amount of coaching can take bad players to new levels—especially if they are unenlightened people who have no desire to make a gut-level decision to *go*.

2. **Do these right players genuinely desire to play at a new level?** Are they hungry, humble, and teachable—or will we spend all of our time trying to convince them they can be better? Will they make a shift in their activity to drive new results (because new results always require new behavior)? You won't see things change if everyone keeps doing all the same stuff they've been doing before.

3. **Do the right players have the capacity to play at a different level?** In other words: Do they possess the knowledge, skills, desire, and confidence to make the important shift they need to remain viable in a changing market? There's nothing worse than having people who either don't want to or can't make this shift on a team whose Leader is tired of subsidizing mediocrity. Sometimes good people just don't have the capacity to do more than they are currently doing. This doesn't mean they're not good people. But we need good people who have the capacity—that is, the ability and the desire—to play at new levels.

Leaving any of the above questions unanswered will likely mean you'll remain stuck and frustrated in a place where too many underachievers live.

I began to understand the importance of having the right Model after spending a decade of my life as a head women's basketball coach. During my 12 years in this field, I turned around a dormant culture with nothing but apathy present and a few minimal signs of life here and there. I eventually learned that the only way to make something important to others is do something so big that people have no choice but to pay attention and take notice. *Life is just too short to think small or become something mediocre.*

During my decade of winning championships and transforming this culture, I began to truly understand that everyone has a ceiling. I also came to appreciate that coaches are the only way that we can break through those ceilings and activate our real potential. Anyone who's ever had a great coach in their life understands that great coaches do three things:

1. They make us **have conversations** we don't want to have.

2. They make us **do things** we may not want to do.

3. They help us **become something** we didn't even think we could become.

Without others' help, all we have is our own ego to convince us that we can make the jump from where we are to where we want to go, and this rarely happens. There are certain gaps or "missing structures" that coaches are trained to recognize and fill to help advance the strategy of the team. As long as these gaps are present the team has underrealized potential and consistently underperforms. One consistent gap is a lack of a clear growth Model that engages every single person toward a dominant aspiration and harnesses the total energy of the group in a coordinated and systematic manner.

This book can become the hammer and nails that you and your group have been looking for to make this shift in your lives and organization. The *Zebras and Cheetahs Model* is predicated on unique experiences of blending coaching acumen with entrepreneurial thinking and using athletic Models to drive business performance and business Models to drive athletic performance. In essence, I've learned how to become a Cheetah and run faster. I've also learned how to become a Zebra and look different from other corporate business folks that one day woke up and arbitrarily decided to label themselves "coach." I am a coach at my core, thanks to the combination of unique experiences and blend of education that's afforded me a differential advantage: the ability to move people through a Model with focus and execution toward a dominant aspiration. You won't hear me use the word goals in this book, as I believe it is the most overused and underdone word in America. People don't reach goals; they lower them. People reach a *dominant focus*, a single rallying cry that drives their own and their group's energy with a laser-like focus and a clarity that achieves greatness. If you don't have one now, you will before you are through reading this book. It's a necessity if you want to thrive in the concrete jungle of the business world.

The Model has helped grow a 2.2 billion-dollar bank by 43 percent in a retail initiative that built 10,000 new customers in the worst economy we've seen in many years. It has also helped to grow a mortgage division by over a million dollars in profit in one calendar year, drive 420 home sales in the worst housing market to date for a home builder, and increase a real estate firm's closings from 120 to 175, making the firm over $400,000 in additional revenue in a one-year cycle.

The lessons this book offers are not only about coaching. They're also about perspective and mindset—which is where Colby Jubenville comes into the equation. As a former coach himself, Colby's perspective and my focus combine to rework your entire outlook—from the way you think, to the way you respond, to the way you experience intentional breakthroughs. Never before have a coach and a strategist come together to form the perfect blend of unique perspective and uncommon focus and execution and achieve such a powerful combination. You can't own a position in the market until you pick one, and Colby is better at helping people find and articulate their position than anyone I've ever known. His unique perspective will launch you on a journey toward differentiation by showing you how to own a space that is suited perfectly for you. You'll need a clear advantage and strategy to survive in the concrete jungle, and Colby provides it.

This book will also explain exactly how to move toward the aforementioned *dominant focus* in your life or business. You'll learn to embrace a new way of thinking that makes you look different, run faster, and stay agile. This Model is a clear way to separate yourself from those around you—to do something that other people seek to replicate.

If there's one thing I could emphasize above all else, it is simply: enjoy the journey. It will change your life and the life of your organization, *if* you're open to what it can offer. One of my favorite spiritual sayings is, "Be open to anything and closed off to nothing." This is where learning and growth start—and where breakthroughs happen.

Coach Micheal J. Burt

Unique Perspective, Then Mindset

I've never met Marshall Mathers (more commonly known by his stage name, Eminem) and I probably never will. But he knows about the concrete jungle in which he lives and has made his fortune rapping about his unique perspective. He sees the world differently than most people do, and consequently he has created a shift in mindset about an entire genre of music. In the song *Love the Way You Lie*, he states, "I can't tell you what it is; I can only tell you what it *feels like*." In his music as each verse unfolds, it's the *feeling* or *emotion* tied to struggle that lets the listener know who he is, what he does, and why he matters.

This got me thinking about where unique perspective comes from, and prompted me to ask the question: How does someone *truly* change their mindset?

One place where a unique perspective originates—at least in my life—has been struggle. Facing hardships has taught me how to become open, humble, and teachable by whatever adversity had to teach me. However, I've found that it's becoming increasingly harder to find opportunities like these anymore. Life in the twenty-first century doesn't really encourage us to embrace, listen to, and learn lessons from struggle. We very rarely take the time to stop and ask, "What is this experience trying to teach me"? Instead, we run toward some finish line that doesn't really exist.

Organizations approach struggle the same way individuals do. Instead of asking the hard questions, we simply accept current circumstances as though we have no control over them, and we tend to blame others for putting us there. Some might find themselves in a life, organization, or job surrounded by a group of people to whom they feel disconnected and wonder how they got there.

But for a select few, a different story unfolds, one whose script comes from their individual experiences and results in a unique perspective. This unique perspective came to me through a few different social intuitions including music and school; however, there was one in particular that I feel provides opportunities for people to struggle, explore, and excel—sports. The games I played with my friends as a child tested my skills and abilities in different ways. They prompted us to create teams of people, all with unique abilities who enjoyed new opportunities to compete every time we played.

I continued to participate in sports through college. Athletics granted me opportunities to learn, grow in responsibility, contribute to a group, and receive recognition. It involved more than simply competing against others and myself; it gave me a chance to gain unique experience. Those moments defined the relationships I made, the people with whom I connected, and the lessons I learned. Eventually, my focus shifted away from the playing field and into the classroom and a unique education. During my graduate work, I began to see how, like a sports team, a classroom had a Leader and a group of followers, all of whom possessed unique skills. Each person did something well, and it was the Leader's job to figure out what that was and how best to put it to use. And the Leaders that managed to do this most effectively were some of the first Zebras and Cheetahs Leaders that I encountered.

Seeing the Big Picture

Zebras and Cheetahs Leaders are indeed special because of their perspective. They see the big picture in its entirety, and they help others see the whole and all its related parts. Consider your own situation. What related parts comprise you, and how are they connected to things around you? One way to discern this is to answer the three big picture questions that I asked myself:

1. Who am I?
2. What am I going to do?
3. Why do I matter to the world?

The answers won't be easy to come by, but they *will* help create some focus, clarity, and direction. They'll allow you to connect the big picture to both the personal and professional elements of who you are.

Tapping into Intensity: Harnessing Your Whole Self

Zebras and Cheetahs Leaders know how to tap into their own intensity to harness the whole self. Of course, this no easy feat; it requires facing yourself, your success, and your failures truthfully, and determining exactly what you're willing to do. Many people go their entire lives without asking these questions, and then they wonder why they ended up where they did. But when you push past your comfort zone, you begin to experience personal and professional breakthroughs—growth you will be able to see, harness, and control. You'll gain a new sense of confidence about your place in the world.

Connecting with the Core

Zebras and Cheetahs Leaders not only understand how to connect to their core; they also know how to help others do the same. This core is each person's unique value— what gives you and others drive and purpose.

The first time I heard Coach Burt speak, I knew that he had connected to his core. He spoke about many topics, but I found myself focusing on and writing down four words: *voice, leadership, execution,* and *culture.* Those core values are the center of what Micheal Burt does, and the legacy that has been created at www.coachburt.com. Identifying these values early in our relationship has allowed us to keep our focus where it needs to be, and it continues to serve as the core from which we work.

Where Do We Go Now?

In the Guns N' Roses song "Sweet Child of Mine" (which has always been a personal favorite), lead singer Axel Rose sings in the chorus, "Where do we go now?" Every time I hear that I can't help but think, that's what everyone wants to know. There's not a person alive who doesn't ask this question, and it's up to the Zebras and Cheetahs Leader to help others figure that out. And, as stated before, they do so by using their unique perspective and experience to figure out what others need, want, can do, and recognize them for their contribution.

My perspective is different from yours, and from that of the next person and the next person. These individual outlooks are what allow us all to share our distinctive experiences and figure out what use they can be to others. Every single one of us has shared some defining moments with incredible people—and along with them teachable moments that bring meaning, purpose, and value in our lives.

And that is essentially why I co-authored this book. Coach Burt and I want to share stories with you that have been with both of us throughout our entire lives. To me, the uniqueness of this book lies in telling this story, one built around something called *collective passion*. It's about the challenges we face as people and as groups and how we connect every day with people, places, and ideas—together. Part stories, part passion, part practice—and all real. It's the struggles that I've already emphasized that are so crucial to our growth. The passion will focus on some of the people and ideas that can significantly shape your thinking; and the practice will come to life through the rituals and routines that bring all of this to life, every day.

My story and life experiences have made me who I am—as yours have likely done for you. They've allowed me to conclude that while we can have *anything* we want in life, we can't have *everything*. That's an idea we all need to understand better, and we hope this book will show you exactly how. It will highlight how your perspective and experience can set you free as you pursue whatever your "anything" is.

Be careful, though, and realize that we can't achieve any great moments in our lives without facing our share of roadblocks along the way. These are the teachable moments that show us life's most basic truths. This book is a reflection of the lessons that our perspective, experiences, education, and interactions have taught us. And with each new experience or lesson came new perspective.

You must know that we all see the world in completely different ways, which has 'created both challenges and opportunities. If you simply slow down and begin to see your world in your own way, reflect upon it, and try to understand what it means, then you'll add significant value to your life and your organization. This book will highlight your ability (and yes, you already have it in you!) to intentionally focus on the steps you need to take to connect to who you are, what you do, and why you matter. It will compel you to articulate your value to the world, and connect the big picture of life to the small picture—*you*.

You will also learn that Zebras and Cheetahs Leaders do three things very well.

They look different. As we all know that's easier said than done. Looking different is more than the culmination of a life; it's a reflection of unique perspective, experiences, education, and relationships. I am a former student-athlete, coach, professor, administrator, and entrepreneur, and each experience gave me an opportunity to see challenges in new ways, as well as to develop a new mindset based on those unique experiences.

They run faster. Training in a way that gives both you and your followers focus and drive is the foundation of this idea. The people we highlight for their speed understand that they cannot give away what they don't possess. They also know that part of being faster is doing things *better.* This is based on the idea that we must systematically develop a set of behaviors that allows us to do something tomorrow that we simply can't do today.

They're agile. They operate according to a way of thinking that focuses on seizing opportunity *in the moment.* It's a mindset that says: competing on commodities instead of distinctive qualities and abilities will lead you to the same dismal place where others find themselves: in a job they hate, a relationship they would leave if they had a chance, and a life that they hoped would be different. This is quite the opposite from what we are frequently instructed to do nowadays: focus on our weaknesses, give into our own insecurities, and accept what every life gives us.

Zebras and Cheetahs Leaders don't do that. They are smarter than that. They know what their weaknesses are and, instead of trying to deny them, they work with others who hide their weaknesses and highlight their strengths. They constantly look to the landscape for new opportunities to provide solutions to the challenges found in those opportunities. In other words, they see the need and they fill it. In order to compete on unique experience, you must develop a new perspective, which drives a new mindset, which delivers new results.

So there it is. Are you ready to jump in and start to compete on something totally different than anyone around you? If so, turn the page.

Welcome to the concrete jungle baby, you're going to do great!

Colby B. Jubenville, PhD

Acknowledgments

Micheal's Thanks

How do you appropriately thank all of the people who help take a project like this from a conversation to an idea to a discussion to a Model and ultimately to a book? To make this book project go it first took people believing in me to give me the chance to lead and use the Model of growth we speak and write about. Wib Evans at FirstBank was the first person to say "I believe in you" and "We don't want you to just speak about this Model— we want you to implement it with our people." From there many enlightened people who saw the value of having a coach in their life have allowed me into their lives with a message that says we can be better tomorrow than we are today with the help of a coach. John Floyd, Pat Weiland, Ralph Huff, Shane Reeves, and Rick Sain, Norman Brown, John Jones, and many other business Leaders have brought me in to coach and develop their people, and for that I'll always be grateful. Marc Fortune has been a tremendous enterprise mentor to me to help take my business to new levels of success and formalize my team. Thank you to Spike McDaniel, my director of operations, for getting me to the many engagements around the world so we can share and impact.

I would like to say thank you to a host of people directly tied to the book. First, Colby Jubenville, the co-author of this book, for believing in a former basketball coach who said we would impact the world, and second, for helping see this project through to its logical conclusion. To Rick Smith who listened to our ideas and gave great feedback including the concept of The Current of the Urgent. To Heather Adams, who connected us with our fantastic literary agent, Shannon Marven at Dupree Miller, and to our wonderful editors, Adrianna Johnson and Christine Moore at John Wiley & Sons, for seeing the value in looking different and standing out. To Joe Calloway, who wrote the forward for the book and for mentoring Colby and me. Many years ago before I met Joe I was using his "Category of One" concept with my teams to speak to differentiation and owning a field versus merely being in the field.

To mentors whom I've met briefly or studied their work and who have deeply impacted my philosophy: the late Dr. Stephen Covey, Randy Gage, Coach Don Meyer, Jim Collins, and Dan Sullivan.

And finally to my support system: Mom, you believed in me and my potential from an early age and watched every game I ever coached. To my good friends Tommy Davidson and Brandon Burks for continuing to have long philosophic discussions about life and success, and to Natalie, the best mom a little girl could ever have and a wonderful partner in life.

Colby's Thanks

Without question this book (and almost all other professional projects in my life) would not have happened without the insight and knowledge of my best friend, Dr. Benjamin D. Goss. I can't say it enough: *Thank You*.

Thank you to Micheal Burt, the co-author and in all cases the *Coach*. Let's get ready to do it again!

Thank you to Heather Adams and her steady commitment to the project. Without Heather we would not have connected to Shannon Marven, Executive Vice President of Dupree Miller and Associates.

To Shannon Marven, thank you for enlightening us to the process and securing the right relationship with John Wiley & Sons.

To Adrianna Johnson and Christine Moore at Wiley, I say thank you. Throughout this project, you proved that editing is truly an art form!

To Joe Calloway, who wrote the Foreword for the book. Your encouragement and advice continue to be at the front of my mind every day. We need to go to lunch real soon!

To Coach Norman Joseph, who took a chance on me and let me be part of one of the most unique opportunities a young coach could ever have. I hope this book is a testament to your ability to validate the worth and potential in others.

To Brian Shulman, founder and CEO of LTS Education Systems, who continues to allow me to be part of the great work he does throughout the country. You, without question, are a Zebra and Cheetah Leader.

To the many people I have worked with or under, including the late Coach Tommy Ranager, Dr. Don Roy, Dr. Jon MacBeth, Dr. Dennis Phillips, Mr. Christer Czajkowski, Mr. Michael Lawson, Mr. Nick Perlick. Each one of you created a defining moment in my life.

Without Ernie Gray, Red Herring Innovation and Design would not be a reality. I thank him for the immeasurable contribution he makes in my life.

And to my high school mentors, the late Coach Bob Rutledge, Coach Charlie Miller, Coach Sandy Santoli, Mr. Pat Taylor, Mr. Charlie Christmas, Coach Andy Robbins, Coach Scott Atkins, Coach Charlie Shipp, and Coach Palmer Kennedy—without you, I wouldn't be who I am today.

To my Mom who sat on our den floor on Hathaway and taught me how to write sentences and later tie ideas together. Without her, I would not be the writer I am today.

And finally, to Katie, who through it all has always been by my side. Together, I think we continue to write a bestseller.

Chapter 1

The Concrete Jungle

This Book's Purpose

Two men—whose names you'll discover later—found themselves at a crossroads in their lives and careers. Upon coming together, they experienced a collision of knowledge, their pasts, and their hopes and dreams for the future. They also discovered that their educational and professional experiences gave them mutual perspective and common ground. As such, they decided to build what many desire to build: something to call their own, but more importantly, something that could impact other people in a powerful way. What emerged from this collision was a Lead that will help individuals change their perspectives, adopt new mindsets, and provide clarity and focus by causing dominant aspirations to become a dominant focus within people and organizations.

If you're not familiar with the terms *dominant aspiration* (and subsequent *dominant focus)*, don't worry; you'll become acquainted with them soon.

The purpose of the book and the Model it describes is to help you formulate that dominant aspiration and focus, specifically by providing a new perspective about how people should be leading and performing within twenty-first century organizations. It will introduce you to a system that, when fully implemented, will give you peace of mind in the knowledge that you have done what you were hired to do: *lead and create a battle-tested tribe of people.* Yes, we said *battle-tested.* However, you'll have to wait to the final chapter to entirely understand exactly what we mean by that term and how to implement the concept within your life and work.

If you just can't wait to find out more about being battle-tested, then go for it—turn to the last chapter! But for those who want to take the journey with us and witness a Model that addresses challenges in the concrete jungle such as having no clear plan to grow, leading to confusion and chaos predicated by the Leader and underperforming teams. Let's take the first step by examining some realities of the organizational messes in which many people find themselves.

A Few Concrete (Jungle) Truths

We realized several truths on our journey in conceptualizing this Model. We believe that it's important that you understand those truths, too, because in the concrete jungle— our chosen metaphor for the typical not-so-orderly modern organizational landscape—there is, alas, no problem-solving magic wand (and no Easy buttons, either).

You have to realize:

- **Just working harder won't do it.** This is an important ingredient to success, but a hamster can work hard running on a wheel, and it won't go anywhere.

- **Just trying your best won't do it.** Let's be honest: sometimes our best alone isn't good enough. We are merely humans, after all, and all of us have at least some limitations in our individual capabilities, particularly when those capabilities aren't aligned in a complementary, synergetic fashion with the capabilities of others.

- **Just using checklists won't do it**. While checklists seem like the perfect tool to get things done, all they really do is allow you to point to an item and say, "We did it." In the end, you probably won't reach a high level of performance, because all you'll be likely to see is a string of unrelated tasks that have left you asking, "*What* exactly did I do? And *why?*"

- **Just using the latest technology won't do it**. We will discuss this trap in depth later but, in sum, don't expect technology to be a fix-all.

How can we tell you that all these things won't work? Because we tried them all, and in doing so, we discovered one ultimate truth: *To truly find a new, higher performance level, you must first change your perspective*. Accordingly, this book is designed to allow you to sharpen your senses so that you can learn the sights, sounds, smells, and, in some cases, tastes and touches of the concrete jungle. Particularly important is

3

The Concrete Jungle

the sense of sight, which, in this case, represents finding your unique perspective. This can happen when you put yourself in a place to receive a new message by becoming humble and teachable, and adopting a mindset that spawns growth.

Don't misunderstand the point about humility. *Humble* doesn't simply mean *submissive* or *reactive*. In fact, examining its root word provides some insight about the source of your unique perspective. The word *humble* originates from the Latin word *humus*, meaning *ground* or *earth*. Survival in the concrete jungle sometimes demands that inhabitants dig deep, past the concrete foundation beneath their feet and into the deepest, richest soil that can provide the growth they need to make new discoveries. Often, many (usually unnecessary) layers of concrete and debris cover this fertile ground. Our point in this instance is to underscore that the foundation upon which you find yourself now standing is a culmination of the life decisions you have made, which brings you to where you are today. Improvement for the future, then, will require that you excavate through the minutiae of your life and (re)discover what makes you, in fact, *you*. This book will help you determine your essence, thereby helping you re-form your foundation for improvement.

Realize, though, that the process of mental excavation is much like the physical one: difficult, gritty, and even painful. However, it's also similar in that the pains that digging causes are well worth the find. And unlike the pain from your current concrete foundation, they're only temporary, not permanent. Either through your current pain or your imagined potential, we hope this work will help you see a new vision of the future and realize that it's time to start digging.

We will help you get started with the "mental mining" you need to do to understand the message in this book, since this will put you in a position to truly comprehend and internalize it. After all, if you're not willing or ready to do the heavy lifting to understand yourself or your career, you'll soon find yourself in a place where you will be left to take only whatever leftover scraps the concrete jungle offers, if any at all.

The Song That Spawned This Book

When we began to discuss writing this book, we revisited a 1987 song from the Guns N' Roses band's debut studio album, entitled *Appetite for Destruction*. We listened to the song "Welcome to the Jungle" and tried to capture the thought process that the band underwent while writing it (as much as we could without the use of certain influential chemicals, of course). Later, we learned that the song was about challenges the band had faced, and the harsh realities of trying to connect their message with an audience while trying to make a living amid the challenges of the music industry.

More than a tale of a band's woes, this song is now a call of the wild in a new jungle—the concrete jungle of many organizations. This is the place where the once-mighty lion is no longer guaranteed to remain king, and where instead a new breed of animal is evolving, one that can adapt to the new environment, gain perspective, then follow an intentional mindset to create a new order from the current chaos.

We call these new animals Zebras and Cheetahs, because they exhibit qualities of both these breeds. Like a zebra, they boast a distinctive appearance that others can easily recognize. Like a cheetah, they possess great speed and are particularly quick accelerators. And like both, they have an ability to utilize their senses so well that they excel in adapting to their environments. Simply stated, they look different, run faster, and are agile—thus, they can escape the chaos around them.

You may currently possess traits of either a Zebra or Cheetah and that's normal. Throughout the book, we will refer to this new hybrid Leader as a Zebra and Cheetah Leader (Z&C Leader). While reading, we challenge you to recognize which animal is a reflection of your unique perspective, education, and experience and possible areas you want to grow that are outside of the instincts found in each. Being intentional about what you want to gain from this journey will help you become the Leader you want to become.

The Concrete Jungle

Chaos? Did somebody say, "Chaos"? (If you'd like, you can re-read that last sentence in a voice like former NFL coach Jim Mora used in his infamous 2001 "Playoffs?!?" press conference rant.)

Yes, we did, and in one word, you've been quickly yet firmly acquainted with that life place we dubbed the concrete jungle. It's a world of incessant phone calls, meetings, e-mails, voice mails, text messages, more phone calls, more meetings, more e-mails, more voice mails, and more text messages, all flooding in from your land line, smart phone, laptop, desktop, and tablet computers, creating what we call the *current of the urgent* (which we'll discuss in more detail later). And don't forget the plethora of social media—Facebook, Twitter, Skype, instant messaging, and so on, that rounds out the technology that amplifies much of the noise we hear in this place. While it's disguised as "getting things done," this noise actually creates a sense of hysteria among organizational members (which we call *the tribe*). Throughout the book we'll be referring to "the tribe" as a group working together through struggle and success. Think of it as a balance between the anthropological definition of tribe and Seth Godin's perception of the term.

There comes a point within a tribe that no one can hear any kind of clear message. You're too busy cleaning out your in-box, deleting and responding to e-mail, and asking yourself why people consistently waste your time with pointless committees and meetings. Yes, we thought you, too, had taken a few swims in the current of the urgent, which drags you deeper and deeper into the concrete jungle.

Complete with its own hierarchy, rules, and terrain, this jungle doesn't simply yield to the roar of the lion anymore. We believe this occurs for several reasons, but the primary one is that the other noisemakers we find in the concrete jungle (including the 10,000-pound gorilla named Culture that you'll meet in Chapter 2) have muffled or even muted this roar. Culture is constantly screeching, beating his chest, and wanting to exercise his power to do what he wants to do rather than what the tribe was brought together to do.

This, in turn, creates a struggle to hear a clear, concise message throughout the tribe. The Zebras and Cheetahs Leader rises above the struggle and noise, leading the tribe through their unique perspective. By virtue of their unique perspective, education, and experience they are the rulers of their tribe and the rulers of the concrete jungle.

Providing clarity amid the chaos requires four things (which we will encapsulate here and expand upon later): *developing awareness* of the realities that the tribe faces; understanding the concrete jungle's *complex order; clearly defining the success* the tribe desires; and *creating a new level of professionalism* that leads to direction and focus. You will gain momentum during this process, with knowledge that the tribe is preparing itself well for life in the concrete jungle. Clarity, direction, and ultimately focus all evolve through the following sequence of four activities:

1. **Developing awareness of the realities faced by the tribe.** Any tribe's natural point of origination is usually to let sheer force determine how

the tribe should exist—that is, who should lead, who should follow, and the precise course the tribe should take. But tribes will not last if they worship sacred cows like easily visible indicators, typical benchmarks, annual performance ratings, or brands that have outlived their lifecycles— all things that may have propagated life in the jungle at one time. Having a dominant aspiration connected to an emotional theme that every tribe member comprehends begins with drawing a clear picture of the true, actual circumstances your organization faces, regardless of how positive or negative they may be.

2. **Understanding the complex order of the concrete jungle.** Tribe members want to know what their future with the tribe will look like. Without this candid approach to reality, their senses will become distorted. They won't be able to successfully confront the vast vacuum of the unknown because they'll be operating according to a non-calibrated sense of what is and isn't real. Individuals cannot survive in the concrete jungle without reliable senses. When they recognize their status as an endangered species, they perceive, in their desperate, disorderly state, a vicious environment where survival is literally impossible at both the personal and organizational levels. The role of leadership within the tribe today is to leverage all members' talents. This requires knowledge of

the jungle, the tribe's systematic core functions, and identification of vested partners who share the same beliefs. All of this enhances the tribe's chosen direction and pace through speed and integration of work initiatives.

3. **Clearly defining the desired levels of success.** Once its members understand the order of the jungle, you will further clarify what constitutes success for the tribe by sharing the unique perspective and mindset that the Zebras and Cheetahs Model creates. You will determine a catalyst for recognizing that success by using a force we call *collective passion*. Why do we use this term? First, the concept of *collective* relates to the whole. Everyone in the tribe is working together within the same context, which in this case is the context of the dominant aspiration. We can view the concept of passion in its modern context, which involves deep affinity for something; however, seeing it as that alone sells the concept short. The word *passion* comes from the Latin word *passio*, which means "to suffer." Therefore, *collective passion* actually involves first the collective struggle, then the collective power found after moving through this struggle to the other side, to a place where you'll find affinity for the tribe and its members. Stated plainly, collective passion helps create a cooperative, unified environment within your organization.

4. **Creating new levels of professionalism.** What exactly will happen when an organization reaches such a plane of passion? Quite simply, the relationship between tribe members will change, specifically in this way: competition *within* the tribe will be replaced by new levels of cooperation. This will then allow the competitive focus to fall where it belongs: *outside* the tribe. You can then base all results on factors within the concrete jungle instead of factors related to the tribe.

Several sociological dysfunctions suddenly disappear when this happens. For instance, tribal members will stop using each other as metrics for their own performances (bringing to mind the old fable of the two bear-chased people running through the woods, each of whom is intent only on outrunning the other, rather than outrunning the bear). Such internal competition, in which members either try to excuse their own inadequacies or backstab those whom they may see as more productive workers, eventually leads to the downfall of the entire tribe (because the bear could easily start chasing the next person once it devours the first one!). Another group dysfunction that will disappear is the trite, pointless end-of-the-year evaluations that provide no clear, accurate sense of tribal members' contributions. And by eliminating that cancer, you subsequently abolish another: a lack of accountability. Why? Tribal members will clearly have their work cut out for them, and their productivity levels will be quite obviously displayed for all to see (bid goodbye to overhearing destructive comments like, "Well, it's almost Christmas, and no one does any real work until after the start of the new year.").

The Relationship between the Jungle and the Tribe: Having, Knowing, Understanding

We once heard a wise Leader tell his tribe, "It is better to know than it is to have; but it is better to *understand* than it is to know." We agreed, and then immediately began to wonder exactly how this applied to us. We didn't truly understand this axiom in the early stages of writing this book. However, as we pushed further into our work, we gained a clear appreciation of how it applied to those desiring to make a shift in perspective and mindset. That appreciation evolved into three clear questions:

- *Having:* Do we *have* a tribe of people with the necessary skills to perform in the needed roles, and are they the right people to continue to perform these skills and roles as we move forward?
- *Knowing:* Without reservation, does our tribe *know* that it needs to shift to a new level?
- *Understanding:* Does our tribe *understand* exactly what it needs to do to make that shift happen?

Individual and Collective Power

This book's power lies in helping you gain clarity, focus, and direction about the Leader in you, the tribe you lead, and principles of a Model that will help your organization deliver on its promise. This precision and drive help to take complicated growth and make it simple, create total engagement, and buy in to the dominant aspiration of the tribe, place tribe members in a structured time and value system resulting in new levels of performance with new levels of engagement, and ultimately incentive people in a systematic way. By developing a system, becoming intentional about the results desired, and understanding the cues from challenges, you can become a Zebra and Cheetah Leader who is ready to craft a message that will create change. If it sounds difficult, you understand it well, because it should. But any worthwhile win in your life will require you to reach past your current state of being and start digging below your foundation to find what lies within you.

Setting the Pace

The pace of the life in the concrete jungle can lead to fatigue and create blind spots among the tribe, which prevents them from envisioning the landscape in its entirety and thus lowers productivity. As such, the Model around which this book revolves demands speedy integration, but not simply speed for the sake of speed alone. We prefer to describe this instead as *deliberate speed*. This is different from raw speed, which can create a reckless sense of confusion. Deliberate speed is rapid, well equipped movement undertaken with a sense of purpose and understanding (as previously discussed). The Zebras and Cheetahs Leader is able to accurately sense when the concrete jungle is dictating the tribe's pace. He or she can then use the Model in this book as a way to infuse speed and integration that connects the essence of the tribe with the way the tribe needs to function.

The Z&C Leader must relate new ideas and methods to make distinctive, positive impressions on customers, while using the principles of accountability woven throughout the Model (and that are very intentional and distinctive, like the stripes on a zebra). In this jungle, speed becomes necessary for the sake of quick, agile, precise movement toward new, fruitful terrain that can provide new opportunities for the tribe (very swift and focused, like the cheetah's movement).

Our integrated Model ties a dominant aspiration (and subsequent dominant focus)—the essence of the tribe—to the channels that deliver it, and illustrates how coaching is needed to create breakthroughs.

Become an Active Participant in Your Own Rescue—And Theirs!

Unfortunately, far too many people are driven into a hysterical state by a lack of having, knowing, and/or understanding. As a result, they are drowning daily in the deadly organizational currents of the heart-of-darkness river of change that flows through the jungle. We will discuss the concept of the current of the urgent later, but for now, just let that metaphor give you another reason why deliberate speed is important.

Learning how to swim next to those caught in the current, while still managing to articulate value and provide solutions that will drive a results-driven rescue, is just as important as completing the rescue itself. It may be even more important in some cases, because drowning people can easily drag their rescuers down with them in fits of desperation. Zebras and Cheetahs Leaders understand the current, how fast it is moving, and its impact in developing and sustaining valuable relationships. This is what will build the trust necessary for effective leadership and subsequent individual and organizational rescues.

Speedy rescues are critically important, since organizations are filled with people who want results but don't know how or where to get them. Most of them have (repeatedly) done the same things in efforts to obtain them: attended seminars, bought books, or took a course (or two, or three, or got a degree, or another degree, or some other educational panacea). Soon, however, the grip of reality started to squeeze them harder and harder: *We must look different from our competitor; absolutely have to be faster to market; and we must be able to change course whenever we find ourselves on the wrong side of the profit and loss sheet*, they realize. What exactly is that realization? That's the current of the urgent—the very real trend that demands that qualified Leaders become actively involved in their rescues. But first, these Leaders must learn how to plan their own rescue while swimming alongside their subordinates in the current.

A Word of Caution

Zebras and Cheetahs encapsulates the lessons from a time when a coach and a strategist decided to look at the world with a unique perspective; intentionally develop a Model that connected vested partners; and help create a new breed of organizational Leaders who understand that an investment in improving those around them is a sound investment in their own success. Our different outlooks provide the basis for our distinctive approach. We each work with corporations, small businesses, and Leaders, Micheal as a coach and Colby as strategist. This allows for each of us to bring our unique perspective (how we see it), unique education (how we know it), unique experience (how we connect to it) to our unique talent (how we deliver it). Coach Burt specializes in coaching and developing talent in a systematic way that allows people to do something tomorrow that they simply can't do today. He learned this skill through the many wins and losses of coaching high school basketball for more than a decade, infusing leadership academies and success principles that culminated in building a championship culture. Micheal retired from coaching in 2008 and his championship culture is still alive and his former school continues to find itself in the championship game or deep in the playoffs almost every year.

Colby, a former NCAA Division III football player, completed a PhD at 27 and wrote a dissertation surrounding the coach-athlete relationship. He initiated a small college football program in 1998 without offices or phones or computers, practice or game fields, uniforms or players—just a dream. Colby was part of a coaching staff that recruited 100 players, was ranked nationally in its second year, and built an organization based on the possibility of what could be. It was during those 20-hour workdays that he learned how to compete on unique perspective, experience, and education. As former coaches in different sports we both have a mindset that organizations need someone to drive the change they seek. Those who lead organizations must have crucial conversations with employees, challenge them to do things they might not want to do, in order for them and the organization to become what they are supposed to become.

Those who read this work will recognize some very powerful, very real, takeaways. You will feel confident in the fact they you're highly capable of changing yourself and the organization you lead. So get ready to dive into a book that mixes stories, passion, successes, and failures, all of which have been drawn from the all-too-real struggles both Micheal and Colby faced collectively and individually. Prepare to read about the harnessed power of collective passion that we've seen successfully bind people and ideas together by challenging existing mindsets of daily rituals and routines of work and life.

But before you go any further, you must know that we see the world differently than we used to see it, with a filter of understanding what it truly takes to win in the concrete jungle. This filter creates both challenges and opportunities. We believe that this book gives us a wonderful opportunity to take the time to share what we have learned with you. If you can take the time to pause, think, reflect, and begin to see the world around you in your distinctive way, the principles this book presents can add significant value to your life and your organization.

What you will take away from this book is the ability to intentionally gain focus on the steps you need to take to connect who you are to what you do, and then to help those in your charge understand why *they* matter, and how they connect, as well.

The time to witness the new kings of the concrete jungle has begun. Zebras and Cheetahs will now reign supreme because they can articulate their value to the world in unique ways and find direction by connecting to the essence found within them and their organizations. They look different, they run faster, and they're more agile than those around them, and none of this is by happenstance. It begins by understanding just as much about yourself as you do about the landscape of the concrete jungle.

Understanding how to become a Zebra and Cheetah Leader begins with a heightened awareness of the competitive advantage that comes from your unique perspective, education, experience, and struggle. Because of your past, you look different from others in the jungle. "Running faster" means responding quickly to new or emerging markets, and "staying agile" implies that you can see and seize opportunity.

Here are five tips for the Zebras and Cheetahs Leader:

1. Use your unique past to help your organization build a bigger future.
2. Look differently at your workplace tribe and the jungle because of the lessons learned. This will result in a new mindset about growth, differentiation, and leadership.
3. Don't wait for opportunity. You should wake up every morning and use a specific growth strategy to take on the jungle that is based on the highest value of your time driven by a dominant focus you want to manifest.
4. Take what appears to be incredibly complicated growth patterns and make them simple, eliciting buy-in from others and removing obstacles for growth.
5. Do not see challenge, only opportunity.

As you further hone your leadership skills, continually ask these six questions:

(*continued*)

(Continued)

1. How is my perspective different from any other in the jungle?
2. Through my education, what do I know that will give me and the tribe an added advantage?
3. What are the top three experiences that have shaped who I am and who I want the tribe to become?
4. What past struggles have helped me think better, make better decisions, and communicate in a way that the tribe understands?
5. Where is the most opportunity for growth for me and my tribe?
6. How can I make all of this simple and easy for others to understand?

Chapter 2

The Landscape of the Concrete Jungle

This jungle is organic—and so is the writing.

We discussed a number of metaphors while writing this book about differentiation and speedy strategic implementation. However, we would always return to a characterization of most peoples' workplace lives as living in a jungle. We knew we were on the right track when we looked up the word *jungle* in the dictionary, because these six meanings are what we found:

1. A wild land overgrown with dense vegetation, often nearly impenetrable, especially tropical vegetation or a tropical rain forest.

2. A wilderness of dense overgrowth; a piece of swampy, thickset forestland.

3. Any confused mass or agglomeration of objects; jumble.

4. Something that baffles or perplexes; maze.

5. A scene of violence and struggle for survival.

6. A place or situation of ruthless competition.

So we continued with the concrete jungle metaphor—a place with which too many of us are familiar, and where too many people remain trapped. This is not the friendly or interesting jungle that we see in Disney movies or on the Discovery Channel. Rather, it's a rough, brutal kind of jungle where the low-hanging fruit has been consumed, leaving only the high-hanging, hard-to-reach fruit that demands both effort and intelligence to attain. Make no mistake, though: you can be successful in the concrete jungle, and that's what this book will help you do. But before you can find your way around, you must learn its landscape in order to navigate your way to success.

Let's be clear: though it is concrete, this jungle is alive with activity (not to be confused with productivity), both in regards to its terrain and the creatures that inhabit it. The concrete jungle demands results forcing those who live in it to determine the highest value of their time in order to be truly productive. Understanding the highest value of your time, you may begin to ask yourself how many times you perform a certain activity each day, week, and month. For example, you may conclude that face-to-face meetings with those outside your tribe is the highest value of your time allowing you to get the results you desire. This revelation will make you ask, "how did I spend my time this week," and "how do I want to spend my time next week"? Those creatures that understand the highest value of their time are the ones who are the most productive in the concrete jungle.

You will meet these creatures along the way, gain insight about how they arrived in the place they call home, and learn why they continue to stay in the landscape that is familiar to them. You will also be introduced to Zebras and Cheetahs Leaders who choose to view the landscape in its entirety, point to a place on the map and say, "This is the way"! The concrete jungle is an organic place where the winds of change, failure, success, and opportunity are always present and blow upon all of us. This chapter will be your lesson in organizational geography. So put on your wide-brim hat (preferably outfitted with some netting), fill your canteen, and lace up your hiking boots. We're about to enter the concrete jungle!

The River of Change

One of the first obstacles we encounter in the concrete jungle is the river of change. For some tribes, this river will flow rapidly, bringing about radical differences over a short period. Management theorists describe this as a changing environment akin to whitewater rapids. Other tribes will see a more gradual flow, in which changes will extend over a longer period, what management theorists label the calm waters metaphor. Regardless of which environment surrounds an organization, change is one constant that we can see in the concrete jungle; tribes and businesses must realize that they will look totally different in 3, 5, and 10 years.

It's important to understand that intentional change takes time and that is something we all wish we had. Be prepared for resistance to the change that is outlined in the Model. It's just the nature of people and the will of the concrete jungle.

Accordingly, the tribes that understand change and become intentional about it will be the ones that will do more than survive; they will continue to grow and thrive. In order for them to do so, they must learn not only to anticipate but to evolve as well. Furthermore, they must learn not only to evolve, but how to evolve *properly*.

Survival in the concrete jungle is not simply based on might and evolution. Instead, the predominant idea of Darwin's survival-of-the-fittest theory of natural selection has faced new levels of unnatural complexity in the office environment.

In the wild, certain tribes have attempted to thwart natural selection with *artificial* selection—that is, breeding for certain desired traits rather than those that are environmentally compatible for survival. This is similar to many organizations that have relied upon the latest technology alone in an attempt to find and fill their niches. This also includes attempts at conservation, or combined scientific, political, and social efforts to stabilize, protect, and preserve an environment despite its evolution or erosion Again, this is akin to the organizational tribes that the concrete jungle has protected, who fear that if the jungle collapses, they will, too. Look no further than the housing market to understand what happens when there is a collapse in the jungle. In the end, those that were left standing were those that were led by people that looked differently at the business and became agile by adjusting to the changing demands of the market.

One such Leader is John Floyd, founder of Ole South Properties, Tennessee's largest independent homebuilder.

Ole South had one of its best years in a decade in 2012 because of the way John led his company through the collapse. John fought with banks to reduce interest payments, refocused his product lines to meet the changing demands of home buyers, repositioned his company, and revamped his workforce in order to meet the change that was ahead of him.

Sink or Swim

Over its 25-year history, Nashville-based Ole South Properties has seen many changes: changes in costs, pricing structure, building methods, customer demands, and the size of its bottom line. In 2010, after hearing Coach Burt speak, John Floyd, decided to make changes inside his organization and asked Coach Burt if he could help.

For many years, Floyd found a way for Ole South to grow its profits, its holdings, and its assets. With a cost-effective building method and homes that suited buyers in all price ranges, Ole South became one of the top builders in middle Tennessee and of the top 100 builders in the nation. In recent times, many homebuilders could not adjust to the new economic reality and decided to exit. Floyd felt the impact as well, but he ultimately decided to confront the new reality head-on.

It was clear to us that from the outset Floyd had a deep desire to own the concrete jungle, much like a coach has a deep desire to win a championship. A championship in sports is easily identifiable: look for the head coach and star athlete holding the trophy at the end of the game.

During our time together we constantly asked ourselves what does a championship look like in the concrete jungle?

In this case, a championship was defined using the Z&C Model: a *dominant aspiration with an emotional pull*. The Model helped define the dominant aspiration, create emotion resulting in a tangible outcome so that everyone could see and know what part they would play in driving toward its fulfillment.

The emotional pull was created through internal and external marketing strategies that released the emotion of the organization. Once the championship level of performance was defined, quarterly campaigns were then created to help everyone stay focused and know their roles on the team.

During our time together, we worked with Ole South on building an aggressive strategy that challenged Floyd on everything from strategy to personnel. The shift in mindset included reframing negative events into trigger events (or events that triggered action into the organization) by using adversity to accelerate the growth of the company and a scoreboard that measured success.

At the conclusion of the first year, Ole South saw the realization of over 300 homes sold in one of the most difficult economic climates in U.S. history. We then shifted our focus to positioning Ole South so that they could compete on their unique perspective and rich history in the middle Tennessee region. Ultimately Ole South survived because of Floyd's ability to change.

Without question, the concrete jungle presents a new selective environment that will lead certain tribes to become extinct because of their refusal to change. Other groups that are ready to claim another's territory at any cost will become predators; and still others will merge into uneasy, unfounded alliances with one another in attempts to become more forceful in the business environment.

Regardless of their approach and efforts to thwart the lightning-fast modern pace of natural selection's brutal forces, an increasing number of organizations will find themselves inevitably swimming in the turbulent rapids of the river of change that flows through the concrete jungle. More specifically, they are feeling the grip of the current of the urgent that we first mentioned in Chapter 1 and will describe in more detail here.

The Current of the Urgent

The *current of the urgent* is the speed at which people can make decisions and the way work flows within an organization. The current is a powerful force that controls much of what receives attention, dictates the tribe's focus, and varies in its pull. It can cause complacency or incite a heightened sense of immediacy in dealing with whatever conditions into which it has pushed tribal members. All living, breathing things in the concrete jungle are connected to the current of the urgent in some way.

There are those who are swimming against the current, those who are floating along in it but with no direction of their own, and sadly, those overwhelmed souls who are about to drown in it. Those swimming against it find that they have the wrong people in their tribe; they go after the wrong relationships, don't understand the concrete jungle's landscape, and are constantly asking, "Why is life in the jungle so hard?" The floaters do all right for themselves, but only for a while. They're really only capable of creating temporary competitive advantages, and they find themselves ill equipped to change when the current pushes them in a new direction or against an obstacle. (These are also the ones who thought a college degree was all they'd ever need, who have failed to become continuous learners, and who found immediate success with no real comprehension of how it happened. Essentially, they're poor environmental analysts.). Sooner or later, these two kinds of people join the drowning individuals described in Chapter 1. They become overwhelmed with the number of phone calls, e-mails, texts, and so forth to the point of paralysis.

Thankfully, though, you and those around you don't have to drown in the river of change or become a victim of the current of the urgent. Those swimming with the current are able to recognize opportunities as they become available. And upon doing so, they can immediately articulate their value to others in the current, which is often the only life vest their fellow swimmers can grab. In other words, if you can't immediately show people how the current of the urgent can work in their favor, they likely won't accept your offer to help them swim with it.

So how exactly can you help show others immediate value? You must contrive the specifics for yourself and your organization, but the general principles are these:

First and foremost, make sure you're offering a life vest to someone *who can, and wants to be, saved.* Most good Leaders want to save everyone, and though a noble sentiment, it is simply not a realistic expectation. You can offer to help all, but realize that not everyone will, or can, accept it.

Second, if you learn to embrace the opportunities change can bring, you *can harness the power of the current and swim with it*, which transforms it into a tool that will do work *for* you. In short, *let the environment around your organization speak to you!* It will provide clues about where you can uncover fertile soil and fruitful vineyards. However, you must learn to systematically analyze it as well.

The third point is: *be a continuous learner*. And realize that formal education is only the beginning. The rest, and by far the most important part, of your education begins *after* the coursework ends. Fourth, *set up effective communications systems* for your organization. Most people would probably say that they possess good communications skills but doubt that others around them are quite as capable in that regard. The fact of the matter is that *all* of us could probably improve in this area. Libraries are filled with reams of information about better communications practices, so avail yourself of them and never be satisfied with the quality of communications levels in your organization; seek to improve it regularly. And fifth, *find ways to eliminate wastes:* time, money, effort, thought, energy—all these things can always be managed more efficiently. What's the connection between eliminating waste and showing immediate value? Very simply: if we eliminate wasteful distractions, suddenly the important things can move more clearly into focus. We will discuss these in greater detail as we continue on our journey.

We've occasionally found in the beginning of any great endeavor that Leaders must actively provide every possible opportunity for their tribes to grab the vision of immediate value. They do this by managing in ways that amount to holding each team member's hand. Yes, it's hard work. Yes, it's time- and effort-consuming. And no, you cannot sustain it indefinitely. But no matter how much of an independent-minded person you may be, wouldn't *you* want a reliable hand to hold until you could pull yourself to safety if you were the one who was drowning? Many times in the workplace employees drown in the details of things that don't help them or the organization become better. The hand that is extended from the Leader is a hand that allows employees to know their role and know what they should focus on. The Zebras and Cheetahs Leader understands when the water is too deep and uses the dominant focus to pull them from the deep water and to a place that allows them to regain confidence and begin swimming again.

However, even once you're out of the water, you're still not out of the woods. If you thought the current of the urgent was a challenge, wait until you confront some of the beasts that roam the landscape of the concrete jungle.

Wild Kingdom: Creatures of the Concrete Jungle

The concrete jungle is filled with those who have refused to adapt to the ever-changing landscape of reality. They have laid claim to their territories, and will fight to defend their way of thinking. They prevent best-practice ideas from getting to decision-makers, and they rarely align performances with expectations. They pass blame from one person to the next, to circumstances, or to sheer bad luck. You cannot miss these creatures; you will see them and notice the unique characteristics that define how they interact with others. During any given day in the office, you may see:

Ostriches: People who bury their head in the sand and don't want to acknowledge reality and challenges they face. You may hear these people say things like, "I choose not to participate in this recession." You also may see them standing around the office talking about the negative aspects of the business or notice that they don't have anything to do with advancing the organization. An ostrich talks the most at meetings in order to give the appearance they are doing things, rarely adding value to the work that must get done. What they don't realize is that simply burying their heads in the sand and waiting for things to blow over won't change the reality. Ignoring circumstances won't make them change or go away.

Turtles: People who want comfort without any risk. This way of thinking leads people to believe that preserving their own comfort outweighs any risk and, as a result, their motivation has dissipated into thin air. You know that place they covet: it's a comfortable place where life is not bad, not fantastic, but *okay*. If circumstances get too uncomfortable for them, they'll slide back into the comforts of their shell and not engage anyone or anything for any reason. And if you threaten them, they'll snap at you. They accomplish things at a painfully slow pace, all the while looking like the weight of the world is on their backs, creating overwhelming difficulty for them to accomplish tasks as simple as putting one foot in front of another (yes, we know plenty of folks like this).

Elephants: People who have strong family ties or other legacies and live in tight family groups called a herd. Though they were previously esteemed for the glamour of their prized ivory tusks, culture and time have made their once-valuable resource(s) dated (even toxic). Thus, embitterment has caused them to develop a thick, calloused hide that makes them impervious to the environment around them. They don't take too kindly to outsiders. They have long memories and will always side with their herd over new ideas. Anger them, and they'll stampede, bringing the entire herd with them against you.

Monkeys: People who swing from tree to tree looking for the next best idea or opportunity without taking the time to really understand how the opportunity will impact them. They're pretty good at imitating what they see, but they have no actual original thoughts, and will gladly steal yours and run away with them. They appear to smile a great deal and seem pretty harmless, but they're quite ferocious when cornered and threatened.

Alligators: People who are threatened by loss of habitat. They are primitive creatures who didn't develop large brain capacities. They therefore possess few instincts other than sheer aggression, the use of force, really big mouths, and sharp teeth to bury into anyone who invades their turf (we wanted to include the problem of not having a toothbrush for all those teeth, but you probably already learned that from the movie *The Waterboy*). Gators are territorial and don't like to interact with outsiders, and their bad attitudes make those around them defensive and aggressive, too.

Lions: People (and even entire organizations) who have been incredibly strong and dominant for very long periods of time and were once invincible, but who have now been outsmarted. Though the strong may have devoured the weak in bygone years, the smart take from the strong in the concrete jungle. Clearly, then, lions are no longer kings of the jungle. They are still powerful, and still roar (think: *noisy marketing campaigns*), and those roars still frighten the not-so-smart tribes. But the new tribes invading the concrete jungle for the first time (competitors) make so much noise that, while the lions are heard, they are no longer revered. And as such, they can no longer solely command attention. Instead, tribes with certain evolved characteristics that better fit the jungle's environment stealthily seize the once-invincible competitive advantages and *market with purpose*; these are the tribes with the lowest cost, the big-box tribes with the best service, the tribes with agile management practices, and so on. During times of drought, developing the tribe's competitive advantage and carefully assessing your paramount competitor's strengths and weaknesses can lead to more than just survival; it can lead to expansion and growth. So don't be afraid of the roar. Listen carefully to it, and then decide how your tribe can exploit it.

And Then . . . There's the 10,000-Pound Gorilla

You've smelled him. You've heard him screech. You've probably dodged a few things he's thrown at you, and you likely have even felt him jump on your back. We're talking about the concrete jungle's biggest brute—the 10,000-pound gorilla named *culture* who will destroy anything in his path, including all of the great ideas that you and your tribe have.

Before we speak further about the concept of organizational culture using this slew-footed metaphor, let's examine some biological characteristics that gorillas possess. In fact, we're betting you'll catch the symbolism from a mile away before we even get to the metaphor's interpretation. Keep a count of how many parallels you find in the next four paragraphs.

Gorillas are extremely intelligent beings who can learn very complex tasks. Humans have successfully taught sign language to some gorillas in captivity, while others have learned how to form simple sentences and communicate with people. Trainers have occasionally observed these creatures using objects such as rocks as primitive tools in the wild, and they have also learned to use various tools in captivity.

Though gorillas are frequently portrayed as destructive, dangerous killers, they are actually shy, passive vegetarians. They live in small groups (or bands) of six or seven individuals. When young gorillas mature, they leave their native band and either join or form another band. Generally, gorillas are quiet animals that communicate with each other using many complicated gestures and sounds. They aren't aggressive. They may make a lot of noise when an intruder disturbs them, but rarely will they confront another animal. And while they can climb trees, they rarely do. Gorillas cannot swim but spend lots of time grooming (cleaning the hair) of other gorillas in the band.

Male gorillas that dominate and lead the groups are called *silverbacks* because of the distinctive ridge of silver fur on their backs. If challenged by a younger or an outsider male, silverbacks will scream, beat their chests, break branches, bare their teeth, then charge forward. A group whose Leader is killed will split and disperse to look for a new protective male, despite the threat that the new males will kill the dead silverback's infants.

Each evening, gorillas construct a nest where they curl up and sleep during the night. They make these bowl-shaped nests from leaves and other plant materials. Only mother and nursing offspring share nests; all other gorillas have their own.

Okay, how many did you count? You probably beat us to the punch, but let's analyze each gorilla characteristic as related to organizational culture, beginning where we ended—with the nesting concept.

Some members of an organization will wonder if culture actually exists at all, because it's often a very covert thing. Some places seldom discuss it directly, because it's not necessarily qualified or quantified; it exists instead as the hefty part of an organization that seemingly hides in plain sight. Yet ironically, if you disturb its nest, the 10,000-pound gorilla called culture will create enough noise that you'll *clearly* know you've crossed its boundaries against its will, and everyone else will know it, too. Typically this is seen in the rising star within the tribe. This person knows what they can be the best at and how to outperform others with more years of experience. But, because of culture, they assume a lower position in the tribe with a designation of "associate," "junior," or "assistant."

When it becomes negative, an organization's culture emits a stale odor (much like an animal's nest). This is one of the first signs that a tribe may have culture-related problems. Progress has come to a stalemate, employees don't want to leave the comfort of familiar surroundings, and they certainly don't want to share their space with anyone.

They actively resist the efforts of those change-brokers who invade the nests (often young and/or progressive-minded employees with positive outlooks and plenty of motivation), and reject their insights. This prompts them to persecute those would-be change-brokers and squash their ideas (For instance, when describing one particularly unsavory cultural group, a colleague of one of ours furiously observed, "They get somewhere, and they just *nest*"! Well stated, because that's exactly what happens). Instead of embracing change and forging ahead into new territories, they'll spend all their time telling each other how wonderful they are and heaping empty praise on others, who in return heap it back upon them. All this does is construct a smokescreen of irreproachability if either group is ever confronted about their lack of productivity.

Rarely will these cultural gorillas engage the difficulty of climbing a little higher than where they are to get a new perspective when they can simply enjoy the comfort of all things familiar on the ground. And forget about swimming in the river of change and figuring out how to harness the current of the urgent: these gorillas would perish if they tried, and they know it. But make no mistake: these are very intelligent people who (sadly) know *exactly* what they're doing with their communications. They are especially talented at making things overly complex and complicated. We've had colleagues like this who'll write reams of pages for policies and manuals, and who'll noisily argue up one side of a discussion and back down another. It's all an attempt to camouflage their true beliefs, confuse those around them, and/or scare away would-be challengers by sounding more intelligent than anyone else. However, when pressed to do so, they won't take a solid stance on *any* issue. These are the same people who want to form committees to address every little thing that the organization encounters, and they love to fall back on concepts like shared governance to try to circumvent responsibility to superiors.

However, the saddest fact of all may be that, due to these aforementioned conditions, the organization's culture collapses upon these individuals if their Leader is removed from the equation. This band of employees (notice we did not use the word *tribe*, which connotes a much more solid attachment to group ideals than the word *band*) scatters, and many probably won't survive without their silverback cultural Leader to watch out for them.

Pretty pathetic, isn't it? Yet all of us can likely at least point to a scenario like this one, and perhaps recall an experience with it, usually because we've been nose to nose with a cultural gorilla on one or two occasions.

You may have also met some of culture's children, or what tribe members may call "the monkey on my back." Look closely, though: these are not monkeys, but rather baby cultural gorillas that will wreak havoc on the tribe. Their names may be familiar, woefully screeching, and culturally shackling refrains such as "Lost," "Hopeless," "Going Nowhere," or "Anywhere But Here." They'll build nests upon finding their way into the tribe, and then have difficulty uprooting them. Why? Culture has trained his offspring well. They won't let go as they become entrenched, because they like to keep their leverage on tribes. And due to their relatively invisible nature, they know that tribe members can't turn around and confront them directly. Instead, the tribe members continue to carry the cultural gorillas on their backs, which incites a great deal of stumbling and frustration.

Tribes that want to find a way to tame culture—to make it productive and civilized (which fortunately *can* be done)—must first acknowledge that they helped feed, nourish, and allow the culture to grow and evolve to its present form. They need culture cultivators (those who are willing to embrace the challenge of capturing and taming the gorilla), who will then retrain, relearn, and activate a culture that gives birth to the potential of the tribe, but not enable culture's offspring. They understand that a domesticated, civilized culture is one in which the tribe does its daily business effectively, even when managers are not around. And they take great pride doing so, because they share passion that keeps them from becoming complacent. They also understand that certain positive and negative organizational cultural elements exist, and they must systematically define those elements so that they can be managed and, in some cases, marketed,

Truett Cathy, founder of Chick-fil-A, is one of the best examples of how culture can be managed and marketed. If you eat fast food, do yourself a favor and go to a place that has a culture unlike any other fast food chain or fast casual dining anywhere. In Murfreesboro, Tennessee, during a Saturday there is a security guard that directs traffic in front of the local Chick-fil-A. They have employees standing before you in the drive-thru line using cell phones to call in orders so that they can extend past their capacity. Employees walk through the main floor offering mints, drink refills, and the chain routinely features family nights with specials that connect with the community. It never fails that children will ask their parents to take them to lunch at the eatery after church. And, every Sunday, disappointed children must choose to eat somewhere else. The culture is intentional; you can see it when you walk through the doors. Entering a Chick-fil-A is like entering a place that is sacred and protected by the culture. It's clean, well lit, with visual cues that teach each customer how they should interact with the establishment. Signs like "Food Is Essential to Life; Therefore Make It Good" and "We Didn't Invent the Chicken, Just the Chicken Sandwich." They even know how to get to the heart of children by allowing them to exchange the books they get with the kids meal. This is a well-known secret inside most kids communities, and parents should be educated about their cost saving tactics as well.

At times, culture works behind the scenes as tribes develop products or services. Yet it simultaneously becomes the very thing that places a stranglehold on the tribe, keeping its rigidity in place and crushing the creativity and risk needed to grow. This rigidity is ultimately what holds the tribe back from becoming what it wants to become. And if the Leader does not take charge of culture, culture will take charge of the Leader! The dominant personalities within the tribe will win, and if these personalities are negative, culture will become negative. Tribes must cultivate exactly what they want to grow; if a 10,000-pound gorilla is left alone to figure it out for itself, the results will be pretty messy. Organizations must identify, define, and utilize culture in the concrete jungle, perhaps with regular sessions that allow the tribe to speak about the realities it faces before culture becomes an unmanageable size. And they must set and manage standards of organizational culture with scoreboard-like precision.

Chants, Dances, and Brands

Tribal Leaders may define culture as *who we are and how we do things*, which is sufficient for examining the organization from an internal perspective. Tribes operating within the concrete jungle must have strong cultures that reflect their differentiating points of view concerning their products or services. They must translate these traits through outward signs similar to tribal chants or dances, activities that answer why they matter and create meaning for tribe members on individual and collective levels.

However, these chants and dances not only carry meaning within the tribe; they also distinguish the tribe among others outside by effectively communicating the things that are important to the tribe (specifically, their values). For businesses, these outward signs are called *brands*. And while they certainly carry great internal meaning, it's equally important for outsiders to understand an organization's culture, because it affects their perceptions of it. In other words, *culture* becomes critical to *positioning*, which is a crucial part of any branding exercise.

Everyone involved in an organization contributes to the size and weight of culture. Help lines, customer assistance, field staffs, and those who influence marketing, public relations, and product development —all of these people have an impact. This is why tribes must first understand the meaning of their cultures, so that they can effectively communicate that meaning to others. Otherwise, customers will not be able to understand it, believe it, or connect with it, let alone form a relationship with it. If a tribe tries to answer the vital questions of "who are we?," "what do we do?," and "why do we matter?," others in the concrete jungle will be just as ignorant about the tribe and its significance. They won't be able to capitalize on investments in its people, and they cannot chant or dance with distinction. And like certain jungle animals, distinction is the whole concept behind the Z&C Leader.

Part Zebras. Part Cheetahs. All Leader.

With all the animals roaming the concrete jungle in their own indistinctive, counterproductive ways—and since the roaring lions no longer can or do rule the jungle—two questions emerge: first, can we find success at all in the concrete jungle? And if so, what kinds of Leaders are necessary to facilitate it?

The answers: yes, we can find success, and the Leaders we need must have the unique qualities to help the tribe look different, run faster, and be agile. To illustrate this metaphor, we researched various jungle animals. We wanted to uncover which ones had the characteristics analogous to that of the Leader whom modern organizations need. And, as you might have guessed by now, we found our Models in the zebras and the cheetahs.

The desired next-generation Leaders combine these two animals' unique qualities—so we named them Zebras and Cheetahs Leaders. These unique qualities culminate in a set of differential advantages that offer different:

- Perspective and mindset (look different, like a zebra)

- Response (run faster, like a cheetah)

- Results (be agile, like both)

However, before we go into detail on how these three qualities emerge among successful modern organizational Leaders, let's give you a quick synopsis of both animals' characteristics. And again, we're betting you'll be able to see the parallels before we point them out later.

Meet the Zebras

Each zebras owns a unique striping pattern; this is what makes it outstanding to its peers, who use these individualized stripes to recognize each another. The stripes also act as a camouflage mechanism in several ways. First, the vertical striping patterns help the zebras hide in grass and deadwood forestry. Although grass and trees aren't white or black, the zebra's main predator, the lion, happens to be color blind, and therefore it cannot distinguish the zebras from the natural cover. And since a zebra typically roams with a herd of other zebras, the multiple stripe patterns confuse predators, since many zebras standing or moving closely together may appear as a single large animal, making it even more difficult for the colorblind lion to identify a single zebra to attack.

Zebras enjoy excellent eyesight, and some experts believe they can distinguish color. These eyes are strategically positioned on the sides of the head, which gives them a wide field of view. Though not as advanced as that of some animals, zebras also have night vision. They also have excellent hearing and can turn their ears in almost any direction, and are equipped as well with acute senses of smell and taste.

Since distance running is a major part of its nomadic grazing existence, zebras have incredible stamina. They're adaptable grazers that can feed off the landscape of many different environments. Although their exact social structure depends on the particular species, zebras are highly social creatures that rely on the other members of the herd for protection.

Meet the Cheetahs

Cheetahs are relatively gentle creatures that will not fight or contest members of their own group. Cheetahs cannot roar but, as highly social creatures, they use other multiple, relatively advanced forms of verbal communication to communicate within the group. It is this ability to communicate that allows the cheetahs to be respected by the tribe. The cheetahs understands how to use its keen sense of composure in moments that matter most. It's this composure or professional calm that allows them to socialize the tribe to their way of thinking.

Cheetahs don't possess the physical prowess or build of stronger jungle cats; however, they are still successful hunters, because they hunt at different times. Though their lean, svelte physiques won't win any grappling matches, cheetahs are built for generating incredible speed. They can run 70 to 75 miles per hour in short bursts and can accelerate from 0 to 64 miles per hour in a mere three seconds. However, their speed would be virtually worthless without feet and respiratory systems to accommodate it. In conjunction with their tails, cheetahs use semi-retractable, cleat-like claws to make sharp turns, which are necessary to out-maneuver predators and prey. Large nostrils and enlarged hearts and lungs work together inside cheetahs to use oxygen effectively and facilitate their blazing speed.

Cheetahs fur has a pattern that makes its spots look like vegetation and flowers to help them blend in until springing into action. They have dark streaks around their eyes that make them look like they've cried rivers of black tears; these tear streaks minimize the glare of sun, allowing cheetahs to stay visually focused while hunting during blinding circumstances.

Meet the Zebras and Cheetahs Leader

Even a casual glance at the characteristics of zebras and cheetahs clearly reveals that they are noticeably different from other animals around them, making them perfect paradigms for our Model.

From zebras origins, Z&C Leaders:

- **Look different**. Just as zebras stripes are distinctive but functional, the distinctive nature of Z&C Leaders will act as camouflage. It helps. The distinction of the stripes on Z&C Leaders in the concrete jungle serves as an identifying trait that allows Z&C Leaders to connect with each other.

- **Stand together**. And when they do so, they appear as one unified, strong organization that's less vulnerable to attacks from competitors.

- **Know the power their group possesses.** When organizations move in a collective fashion, competitors have difficulties anticipating their next moves, which give them a clear advantage.

- **See opportunities.** This ability to see clearly and distinctly with unique perspectives and wide views of the world puts Z&C Leaders in positions to scan their environments for opportunities that others may not see.

- **Can even see opportunities in dark conditions.** The advantage of seeing opportunities even in the darkest of times and through the most difficult of circumstances will help Z&C Leaders gain competitive advantages until conditions improve.

- **Clearly hear important messages above the din.** Contrary to what some may say, we don't live in the Information Age; we live in the Information *Overload* Age. It's not just about information in the concrete jungle; it's about finding the *right* information. Tuning your ears to the right information is a valuable skill.

- **Use all senses and can therefore adapt more readily.** There are times when *intuition*—or instincts based on past experience, feelings, and emotion— may be all that Z&C Leaders have to guide decision-making (much like the senses of smell and taste). While certainly not as solid and logic-driven as sight and hearing, these finer senses may be what separate Z&C Leaders from competitors when nothing else is available, or when everyone else has the same information. These secondary senses can also allow you to change more readily and comfortably according to surrounding conditions. Furthermore, thinking logically may be a mistake when negotiating a deal or formulating a strategy. Instead, sensing how or what the opposition thinks or wants may position Z&C Leaders better than using hard data or reason.

From cheetahs origins, Z&C Leaders:

- **Use unique characteristics and even apparent disadvantages to create advantages among**

peers. While perhaps not as powerful or resource-rich as competitors, Z&C Leaders will create opportunities where none exist. They do this by using what's at hand, in a different way than others use it, or in a way that has never been done.

- **Don't need to roar to command the attention of others.** Because they are gifted communicators, Z&C Leaders can use emotional persuasion that's rooted in collective passion that will eventually win over even the most difficult people. This allows communication to originate not from places of fear, but from a place that helps others clearly understand and form connections with them.

- **Implement new strategies with blazing speed.** Z&C Leaders are the first in the concrete jungle to seize the next great opportunity. They can use speed of integration as an advantage, primarily thanks to their superior knowledge of systems.

- **Not blinded by distractions.** Sometimes their hard-earned marks of tear streaks from past frustrations and failures can keep Z&C Leaders from becoming distracted by unimportant factors that can wreck long-term vision and short-term strategies. In essence, experience has made them able to keep a long-term view.

- **Built for agility to seize advantages the landscape may offer.** Z&C Leaders avoid over-committing to too many initiatives, or falling victim to escalated or failing ones. In this way, they're able to nimbly outmaneuver their competition as the landscape and conditions of the concrete jungle may dictate.

- **Use systems.** No single element of the organization can exist in its own orbit, and no person is an island. Z&C Leaders design, develop, and implement systems that work to effectively and efficiently coordinate and integrate the inputs, throughputs, and outputs of the organization, and to put people in positions that meet their passions and talents. This systematic approach is the basis for the Z&C Model that we'll discuss in great detail in Chapter 5.

Size Doesn't Matter

The one variable that didn't emerge as an important characteristic when researching animals for our Model was *size*. In fact, we found that other variables are much more important. So don't worry; at no point in this book will we talk to you about upsizing your organization. The Z&C Model is for small organizations, large organizations, and all sizes in between.

However, we must provide caution about one thing: regardless of your organization's size, you had better be armed before you enter the marketplace. After all, it's a jungle out there—a concrete jungle! Preparing to venture into it should not be taken lightly, because one thing is clear in this environment: those who do so will need new skill sets and new tool sets to survive and eventually thrive. These new skills and tools that are developed during the implementation of the Model allow us to adapt to the changing landscapes. Whether its through sudden bursts of energy that awake the tribe, addressing levels of performance found in the tribe, providing systematic coaching for the tribe, and having a scoreboard that lets everyone in the tribe know where they stand, a dominant focus helps the tribe articulate its value in new ways, and align with new resources and tools we find in the jungle. But as you probably already know, few people, no matter how talented, can forge their own ways in the concrete jungle by themselves. They must have someone to help navigate through this jungle; *they must select the right Leader.* We trust that the information in this chapter has helped shape your thinking about general characteristics that will help you and your organization do that, and perhaps even help you make the shift to becoming one. We will further refine this concept as we move into other chapters, but before we do, let's address some concepts about an effective Leader who's built for today's concrete jungle.

Looking different is about understanding your unique past, including unique experiences and education, then using that to answer the most important question: where is there a need in the world that only I (or my product or service) can fulfill? We call that unique value.

Look Different

Few companies have a challenge as difficult as TRICOR, a self-supported government agency located in Nashville,

Tennessee. Led by savvy CEO Pat Weiland, TRICOR is focused on helping prisoners get out and stay out of prison. Using the acronym "GOSO," the Get Out and Stay Out program focuses on a unique blend of personal development, coaching, job skills, and curriculum instruction to rehabilitate and decrease the recidivism rate. TRICOR was looking to build a culture with a systematic Model of growth and improvement, essentially turning managers and supervisors into coaches. This was a total shift in how TRICOR previously looked at management. Armed with the Z&C Model, each manager and supervisor began to look at their roles within the organization differently.

Here is what the process looked like:

- Create a dominant aspiration that was clear and bold, which was "Get Out and Stay Out," or "GOSO."

- Develop a theme that elicits an emotional pull. For TRICOR, that was to use the concept of GOSO to decrease the recidivism rate while also showing a profit for the "double bottom line" of their company since they were self-supporting.

- Start with a motivational rally to engage TRICOR's people and get a buy-in to the coaching. This opens the minds and the hearts of the people and reengages the culture.

- Begin the coaching process on personal development, leadership, sales systems, and culture in a systematic way with a proven coach and a proven system.

- Create a scoreboard that tracks daily progress toward the dominant focus in sales. Place people in a high-value activity system that aligns their time with best strategies, thus eliminating the dreaded time-management issue.

- Coach the heck out of everybody with intensity, a focus, and a specific curriculum that develops all parts of each person's nature: body, mind, heart, and spirit.

- Implant thunderbolts as needed. These sudden bolts of energy will keep people focused on the dominant aspiration.

- Become the change they seek by decreasing the GOSO rate and showing more financial profitability.

TRICOR is an example of an organization that adopted an entrepreneurial mindset and executed it. When focusing on results and not time, the potential of people can be multiplied. The TRICOR plan called for a multiyear process of engaging the hearts and minds of the employees (those that work with the offenders) in such a way that they become vested partners and coaches to those they are supervising. TRICOR replaced the old command-and-control mindset of supervision with one of growth and improvement of coaching and feedback by using the Model.

Choose Well

Like many people, you may frequently ask, "What exactly *is* great leadership, and why is it so difficult to lead today?" The bottom-line answer is this: people in organizations today have been turned loose to survive in organizational environments that are as wild as jungles. If someone doesn't have the character and the competence to lead, the jungle will quickly reveal those weaknesses. Therefore, if your organization can't find a guide who will provide the necessary leadership, you may consider arming yourself in other, more dangerous ways of self-protection. But what is your weapon of choice? Simply borrowing strength from a position of power will leave you in a very difficult place; like a gun, it can backfire or be used against you. The jungle is a place where big-barreled weapons won't help you as much as you think.

The reason why is fairly simple: the concrete jungle doesn't just require strength, or having a strong mindset (remember what we said earlier about the Darwinistic evolution of today in which the smart are taking from the strong); it's about *changing your mindset*. Simply waving big weapons (or roaring like a lion) is not a viable, long-term solution. To see real change, you must remember that the concrete jungle rewards and celebrates uniqueness in tangible, recognizable ways, and that today's marketplace climate demands it.

All things in this jungle gravitate toward the call of leadership. So be sure to choose well, since the concrete jungle is a place full of fear, change, and risk. However, it's also a place that brings countless new opportunities for you and your team to experience defining moments—opportunities to look different, run faster, and become agile. This is the leadership imperative of the twenty-first century, and it happens because Leaders develop new perspectives that generate new mindsets.

In a few chapters, we will introduce you to the Z&C Model that will facilitate accountability and drive the results of your people and your organization. However, before we do, we need to rewire your thinking a bit to put you in a position to truly understand the Model.

So, as the sun sets on the concrete jungle, stop, reflect, and make a conscious decision to make the shift toward effective leadership, then remember its ingredients: new perspective first, then a new mindset.

Are You Zebras or Cheetahs or Both?

Understanding which leadership qualities you gravitate toward will help you become the kind of Leader your tribe will follow and the jungle will revere. Think about which of the following qualities best describe your approach to your workplace dynamic.

Those from Zebras origins:

- Look differently, at themselves and their business.
- Stand together, even in the most difficult of circumstances.
- Know the power the group possesses, and use it.
- See opportunities, not challenges.
- Use all senses and therefore be able to adapt more readily to change and to people.

Those from Cheetahs origins:

- Use unique characteristics and even apparent disadvantages to create advantages among peers. What others see as a threat, you see as a challenge.
- Don't need to roar to command attention of others; it's about a professional calm.
- Implement new strategies with blazing speed that is focused on the next big opportunity, faster to market.
- Not blinded by distractions; laser focused on execution.
- Built for agility to seize advantages the landscape may offer, by not saying yes to every opportunity.
- Use systems to create change. Each system has an input, a process, and an output.

Chapter 3

You and Your Tribe

Struggle in the Jungle

It will take time to adjust to the surroundings of the concrete jungle. Faced with a struggle for survival at one time or another, many in your tribe will want to walk (possibly run) away from the change that is about to take place. If current methods that the tribe is using have failed to produce sufficient results, it's only natural that there must be a change.

As you certainly know by now, it is highly likely that change will initiate fear, and rightly so, in most cases. Perhaps you're tackling a new product offering or a different way of doing business. Such circumstances require a Leader who can effectively keep members from bolting, give them a credible reason to continue wrestling with their environment, and reassure them that they will realize ultimate triumph if they work together toward a collectively prized outcome (swimming alongside them in the current of the urgent, as we described in the last chapter). As a result, Leaders must invest serious time in tasks that might seem a little like babysitting—that is, until their subordinates become acclimated enough to the environment to struggle against it independently.

In fact, the initial four to six months of the change process will likely be the rockiest period for Leaders. This is when they'll attempt to design, develop, and initiate successful change without alienating the organization's members individually or collectively, all while keeping them moving forward until they buy into the plan for the future.

Such a situation puts Leaders into a conundrum of epic proportions by forcing them to discern which employees are worth nurturing and which are not. And how can they move those worthy of nurturing from a state of helplessness to one of capability? This chapter will help you address these vital organizational questions from a Z&C Leader's perspective.

Summoning Courage to Lead

We've learned throughout our careers in business, education, and coaching that many Leaders choose not to confront problematic individuals or address difficult issues. Instead, they look at change as an opportunity to set a strong tone with their tribe.

We frequently see institutional Leaders who simply lacked the courage to take firm stances against certain unacceptable behaviors or production levels. They might not realize it, but by allowing this, these Leaders failed to send a clear message that such activities would not be tolerated. These Leaders are much like a sales manager who recruits salespeople who fit a profile that he is comfortable leading, rather than asking what kind of person would customers respond to best. The sales manager in essence holds the organization hostage. The Leader knows it, allows it to go on, and sends a message to everyone else in the organization, but it is the wrong message. Consequently, employees look at each other and say, "that's just the way it is." And there it is. Death by leadership.

However, while management may find it difficult to send such messages, we've seldom observed any athletic coaches with qualms about it. Observe virtually any sporting event, at any level of competition, for any length of time. You'll quickly see coaches remove players who don't follow instructions, or who underperform, and relegate them to the bench. They realize that all players' efforts must be wholly committed to the game plan and yield a certain level of productivity—otherwise, the team has no chance to win. Furthermore, coaches realize that they bear the direct responsibility to correct dysfunctional or lackluster efforts. They're also aware that their abilities to do so effectively are publicly visible for judgment. They must therefore lead with a fair but firm and fast hand, and their players must realize that they cannot play with their own agendas in mind. Why should this apply in a professional setting? Imagine you walking into your meeting and saying, "Mr. Sessions, we won't tolerate your lack of performance anymore and have assigned Mr. Sayers to your position." How would that impact the mindset of your people?

It seems like an elementary concept when analyzed from a sporting perspective. Yet this management practice is quite underutilized in far too many organizational settings. Rather than "bench" insubordinate and ineffective employees, many business Leaders allow employees to do as they please. Companies thereby *encourage* the dysfunctional behaviors by permitting their existence in the workplace, and essentially they subsidize mediocrity in the process. Such organizations will not last in the concrete jungle, and Z&C Leaders understand that conflict is part of the change that must take place. Summoning the courage to act becomes paramount, as Z&C Leaders realize that change begins only when they initiate it.

While such a realization is critical to survival in the concrete jungle, Z&C Leaders must also be armed with an understanding of several other principles that will increase their confidence and ability to act effectively when leading their tribe. Most coaches begin training regiments with running exercises, and Z&C Leaders should be no different. Just like the folks with the whistles, they must coach their followers how to run, as well as toward and from what.

Courage Means Going First

Nobody understands courage better than Chief Administration Officer (CAO) Wib Evans of FirstBank, a $2.2 billion independently owned bank in Tennessee, under the mentorship of bank chairman Jim Ayers.

In the fall of 2008, Wib Evans opened a dialogue with Coach Burt about launching the largest retail initiative in the bank's history. The dominant aspiration was to open 10,000 new checking accounts across 40-plus cities served by the bank, which owned $2.2 billion in assets.

After several meetings with key bank personnel, the need clearly emerged for a new kind of Leader or coach who could help drive the process, implant systems to win, motivate, and inspire the associates, and instill the laser-like focus needed to achieve the lofty target.

In October 2008, Coach Burt began planting the seed for what was to come in 2009 with a tour through the branches in all FirstBank cities, attending the bank's leadership training sessions, and working with bank Leaders to implement the Z&C Model. At that time, Colby created an emotional theme around "RockStar Management," and its focus was to encourage associates to become rock stars of the banking industry with a new perspective about the role they played in the bank and a new mindset of becoming the best at what they do. With new incentive systems, rewards for performance, statewide motivational trainings, and a scoreboard mechanism that measured weekly performance of every branch, FirstBank associates officially hit the seemingly unachievable number of 10,000 new accounts.

Leaders who have courage understand that part of leading is recognizing any missing components that impede the group from performing.

Courage in your organization can be seen by:

- Asking probing questions of your people and actively listening and acting.

- Understanding that leadership is about coaching of talent and potential, not control.

- Constantly paying attention to your senses to detect opportunity in the market.

Running as a Way of Being

During the time of transition from schooling into pursuing professional endeavors, most of us paint a picture in our heads of what our future will look like. We imagine getting our first job and then making a steady climb up the ladder. In an effort to prove our worth, we do everything we can to move up as fast as possible—so we start to run. Unsatisfied, we run a little faster. Then we run faster still. Pretty soon, we're tired, and we don't have much (if anything) to show for all our running.

Motivated by the few results we might have accumulated, we figure that we can prove our worth if we can do more of the things that yielded success.

So we run a little faster.

If or when the results stop coming, we scramble to try something different to (re)produce success. Without finding success, we become frantic as time passes, and we begin to run as fast as we possibly can, and in any direction toward which we may see a little light. But the next thing we know, we've run headlong into a trap.

Z&C Leaders understand that when people spend count-less hours practicing their art, they tend to carry more advantages with them through life. Some people's awakenings occur during their formative years, while others awaken when in high school or college. Still others have awakened after running for what seems like an eternity. Some of the greatest performers experienced breakthroughs only after many years of practice, just as we did as coaches. What if you woke up one day and money didn't matter?

You didn't have to pay the next car payment, house payment, or dental bill. And you could pursue any career path that you wanted. What if you didn't participate in something called "The Big Lie" where your parents or friends told you that if you simply went to college and then got a job, life would be okay?

You stop running by finding your voice. Voice, as we discuss later in the chapter, is the intersection of talent, passion, conscience, and need in the world that only you can fulfill.

Passion can be defined as something you love so much you would drive three states over to talk about it for free. Early in both of our careers we worked for free (or almost free.) Coach Burt started his coaching career at Woodbury Grammar for $295 a season. Colby began his career as an assistant college coach, initially volunteering, and he lived in a vacant dorm for six months before signing a contract. Some may call that foolish, but we call that passion.

The concrete jungle has a cruel landscape, and if you don't pay attention, you will find yourself running without a purpose, too.

Running with Purpose

Running faster is more than just reacting to the demands of the concrete jungle or outworking the competition. It's part of what's needed to dominate in the concrete jungle and it's about running with a purpose. Those who run with a purpose:

- Understand the highest use of your time.
- Have knowledge of the market and the competition.
- Know how to articulate value proposition.
- Know how to overcome objection.
- Have a willingness to develop new capacities.

Daily activities that help you run faster include systematic ways to attack the concrete jungle by:

- Time-blocking.
- Leading your tribe through shared mechanisms so they can gain knowledge.
- Having Monday tribal council meetings, Wednesday education sessions, and Friday autopsy sessions (to understand what has been hunted or what is hunting you).

Running faster can culminate in many different activities for you. To find out whether you are running faster, ask yourself if you:

- Have a coordinated plan that joins the highest use of your time toward a dominant aspiration.

- Have a specific time daily that you work in your business by doing activities that create new business.

- Seek new education opportunities by constantly growing yourself and your tribe in order to leverage their talents.

Run Faster than the Media

As the CEO of the Better Business Bureau of Middle Tennessee, Kathleen Calligan has a reputation of building an organization with integrity. Kathleen has been the voice of the bureau for many years and is an advocate for the important role it plays in how businesses conduct themselves and interact with customers.

In 2010, she illustrated how a Leader can run faster when ABC's *20/20*, a TV news magazine, aired a story that, in her opinion, painted a distorted picture of reality. Upon the airing of the story, Calligan leaped into action, but not by simply reacting to the media and stating, "this is false." Rather, she used her deep understanding of the markets and the people that the BBB served to overcome this unsubstantiated objection. For Calligan, it was not a crisis where she had to react, rather an opportunity to tell the story of the BBB in a way that illustrated its true collective passion. She dove in the current of the urgent, summoned the organization's unique perspective and experience, and crafted a press release that articulated the real value of the BBB while simultaneously separating fact from fiction. The release provided insight to the media, its members, and the public by focusing on the real issue, which for Calligan was and has always been defining the true value the BBB brings to its members.

At the conclusion of her press release Calligan stated, "What distinguishes BBB Accredited Businesses isn't writing a check. It's their desire to be affiliated with an organization that has championed ethics in the marketplace for 98 years and to support its efforts to expose the bad businesses that victimize their employees, customers, family, and friends. What distinguishes BBB Accredited Businesses is accountability with substance."

The phrase "accountability with substance" became the collective passion that meaningfully connected the BBB, its employees, and customers.

The Con of the Concrete Jungle: The Greatest of Traps

This is a real phenomenon, as well as something that most of us have experienced at some point in our professional lives. This "Con" we speak of refers to a vicious cycle that happens as in the following five steps.

1. You find a job in an organization that welcomes you in, provides relative comfort (at least in the form of a paycheck), and allows you to survive.

2. Eventually, a comfortable survival ceases to exist for one or more of a number of basic reasons:

your lifestyle or economic factors render your paycheck inadequate; you become dissatisfied with your personal growth path or capacity; you have good ideas that could benefit the company, but you cannot bring them to fruition; you suddenly lack the resources needed to effectively do your job; the organization changes its movement in a direction with which you are uncomfortable, don't really understand, or disagree; and/or you find yourself under the supervision of a poor Leader, and you feel underutilized, undervalued, and underappreciated. One or more of these conditions thus ensnares you, creating a sense of discomfort and dissatisfaction that grows (rapidly) with time.

3. The harder you fight against the ensnarement, the tighter its grip becomes on you. You still don't get a raise; you still can't get anyone to listen to you; the lack of productivity threatens your existence in the organization; overall organizational floundering and/or cornering by a poor Leader endangers you and everyone around you, turning everyone into savages who'll do anything to survive.

4. Frantically searching every classified ad and online job board you can find, you identify a position in another organization for which you're qualified, manage to obtain an interview, nail it, and get a new job, thinking, *This time, things will surely be*

different! Finally, you feel that sense of comfort you'd had before.

5. Then suddenly, you're back to #2, then #3, then #4 again. And again. And again!

Now you know why we say that you have been trapped and deceived by the Con of the concrete jungle.

Perhaps this cycle repeats itself for you every three to five years. While that may sound a bit exaggerated, statistics tell us that the average American employee will change careers eight to ten times throughout their professional lives. Other statistics tell us that more than 50 percent of Americans claim to be dissatisfied with their jobs (so if it's not you, it's the person sitting next to you!). We encourage you to do your own informal polling to see what you find, and we're willing to bet that you'll get pretty close to 50 percent, too (if not more).

What does this cycle say about the strength of this conning trap, and how can we run away from it? That begins by understanding the relationship between two very similar-looking words: *values* and *value*.

Value and Values: How to Live the Tribal Story

The typical path for most of us goes something like this: attend college or some other form of schooling, obtain a degree, interview with as many companies as possible, and land a job—*any* job. We hope that someone out there will see *value* in our pedigree and talents, and that's important; we *do* need to possess some skills/abilities for which someone is willing to pay.

However, *value* is only part of the process of avoiding the trap. Many of us fail to realize that creating value can only evolve from a shared concept of what we consider important. Said another way: if something is important to one person, another person must also find importance in it if they are to both agree on its value. Said still another way: *values* dictate *value*. Therefore, before a person can create *value* for an organization, that person's *values* (what s/he finds important) must align with the organization's *values* (what the organization finds important).

This inability to distinguish between *value* and *values* may explain why the Con is such a powerful force: too many individuals stumble upon it only half-armed and completely unaware of their incapacity to avoid it. It's happened to us, and it's probably happened to you, too. Reflect upon when you started your professional life. Did you focus on the *value* you added to the tribe, or were you also attracted by the *values* that connected something inside of you to the tribe? Most people, including us, focused only on *value*. Why? Because we typically hope that our higher education (four-plus years of life) and our related work experiences will translate into some relative worth, merit, or importance that helps define us and shape how others see us in the workplace. As these educational and experiential elements increase, so goes our expected level of value. We expect others to readily observe and appreciate this value for what it's worth. We also assume that it will be our ticket to a higher level. In other words, we presume that someone will see value in who we are and what we offer, giving us credence as to why we matter to the world.

Unfortunately, that's the trap at work at its most devious level. Instead of actively searching for a place where we fit, we passively sit waiting, *hoping* to be discovered. Then we are laboring alone in an isolated corner of the concrete jungle and have not attached ourselves to a tribe. Can we survive in such a place on our own? Obviously not.

Clearly, then, we must expand our knowledge of *values* to better understand our tribe, its purpose, and where we fit within it. Here are some good questions to ask yourself in an attempt to begin that quest.

Values

- What exactly is the essence of your tribe that makes it what it is? (core values)
- Why does your tribe matter? (purpose)

Value

- What things does your tribe possess or have at its disposal? (resources)
- What exactly does your tribe produce? (goods or services)
- How does your tribe produce its products? (process)
- How is the value created unique?

As we explained, many people spend most of their time focusing on the last three questions and very little on the first two. This is because the last three translate into specific, highly scrutinized measures of *value* or worth (i.e., they are quickly and readily related to the bottom line or the top line), whereas the first two (*values*) focus on the tribe's core principles or collective passion, and the reason for its existence. However, if you don't answer the first two questions, the last three have no relevance when the jungle becomes chaotic because *values* should dictate *value*. If these two are disconnected, individuals can easily become intentionally or unintentionally cut off from the tribe, leaving them to fight alone for survival.

This is a pretty thick concept to absorb, so mull it over for a while. Once you begin to absorb it, we believe you'll immediately start to understand not only why so many individuals find themselves ostracized from the tribe, but also why so many Leaders prove to be ineffective: *They simply could not generate* value *because they could not bond with their subordinates around a set of core* values. Then what? They couldn't think about their own personal and professional lives—much less other people's—in a different way. They couldn't answer: *Who am I?* or *What can I do?* and *Why do I matter to the world?* Nor could they help those they were supposed to lead in finding answers to the same big-picture questions. Accordingly, no connection existed among and between the tribe, its members, and its Leader. And they perished in the trap laid by the concrete jungle, even though they may have been running at full capacity. As former coaches we both understand the concept of values as things that are, as Jim Collins says in *Good to Great,* "always present but never perfect." It's these values that shape the relationships we have, the decisions we make, and how we choose to spend our time. One thing we both value is a concept rooted in the idea of using adversity to accelerate growth. What if you got to a point in your life where adversity became the very fuel to drive you to not make the same mistakes, not go down the same road, and create a better plan for the future? We both did, and we use that to drive us to the dominant aspiration we have in our lives.

This distinction of value and values becomes so clear as we progress through our professional lives that, at some point in our careers, we say something like, "I would never work for (insert name of the company where you had your first job) again for any amount of money." At that point, we've recognized the Con and the difference between our focus in the early stages of our career (*value*) versus in the second and third phases of our careers (*values*). This is when we can finally begin to answer those big-picture questions of who we are, what we do, and why we matter. And what we originally thought to be a priority in the initial stages of professional life—*value*—takes a back seat once we've learned to focus on *values*.

Core values allow Z&C Leaders to connect with tribe members. They also allow the tribe to find its unique voice, share a story with others, and close the execution gap—that is, the space between thinking and doing—all while creating confidence within the tribe as a whole and its individual members. Suddenly, the members of the tribe stop running at random and *away* from the trap and instead run toward something that matters, that they clearly see, and that they find important.

People: The Life Force of the Jungle

The decision to become a Z&C Leader usually comes as a result of experiencing either pain or potential. These are instances during which people decide they're dissatisfied with current results or are seeking better ones. Z&C Leaders understand that they've been hired for one reason: to achieve new results. But in order to do so, they must figure out how their values connect to their behavior *before* bringing their messages to their tribes. The reason for this is simple: *Even these special kinds of Leaders can't be successful by themselves.*

When companies begin seeking new behaviors to drive new results, they need someone with an entirely unique perspective to help them do so.

They need a Z&C Leader who has enough energy to awaken employees' spirits and remove them from their complacent states, as we discussed before, and who can give them a place toward which they can successfully and confidently run. Companies these days will pay for this kind of positive energy, which can actually be described as a commodity in today's economy. They seek out the individuals who make conscious decisions to have positive dispositions and radiate energy. Operating with the knowledge that people have this kind of potential energy inside them, Z&C Leaders aim to find it and release it. By doing so, they're recharging the bases of each employee and of the company.

People warned us when we began our speaking careers that audience members might not remember what we said, but they would *definitely* remember how we made them feel. That's why we focus on bringing high-octane energy with a contagious passion.

Employees who are ensnared in the trap we just discussed often fall victim to the emotional cancer of complacency, which results in low energy and even lower morale. However, the greatest danger may be that, in many cases, they may be oblivious to that state; in others, they may be aware of it but unsure of its origin.

However, things can change when Z&C Leaders become a part of the equation. They begin by asking employees probing questions (which we will discuss soon) in order to understand why they selected their chosen profession. They dig to find out whether they've lost their passion and are operating under negative mindsets. Because they generate the answers simply by asking individuals to look *inward*, these leaders can accomplish two things; they can take humble and teachable employees to new levels, and they can identify uninspired employees who drain resources from the tribe.

These Leaders are also aware that they can only win by believing in their own abilities to do so. After all, how will others be inspired by an uninspired Leader? Yet too many business professionals are self-defeated from the beginning. They use the unsteady economy as an excuse to be lazy while waiting for the market to bounce back. Other industries like education don't offer incentives for teachers to be remarkable, thereby encouraging teachers to simply mark time instead of attempting to educate students. The concrete jungle remains littered with the corpses of those who didn't have a Z&C Leader to help them avoid the Con of the concrete jungle. Z&C Leaders are different. They recharge their employees and ignite their forgotten passions, a process that involves much more than waving a magic wand. They must make a concerted effort to alter these individuals' perceptions about work by supporting a fundamental shift: to have their work be driven by passion rather than finances. Frederick Herzberg, American psychologist and management guru, focused on job enrichment as the key to getting people excited about their work. His motivation-hygiene theory helps Leaders see factors that truly motivate the work force are found in doing the work, and that dissatisfaction in the workplace comes from another set of hygiene factors surrounding the work, including company policy, supervision, salary, status, interpersonal relationships, and job security. Igniting passion in others can be done by providing your tribe with the following things:

Opportunities to learn in their current role.

- Growth in responsibility in order to lead others.

- Contributions to the tribe in a way that matters to them.

- Recognizing them for the great work they do!

We kick off what we do with organizations by holding motivational rallies. This serves to recharge and excite employees and to solicit their buy-in. But we don't just stage a pep rally filled with lots of cheerleading, confetti-drops, and pep-band music.

Instead, we clearly communicate the things that are important about the new campaign, and how those things relate to what employees have told us is important to them. Like a team with a losing record, they need to believe that their coach is capable of turning things around. Only Z&C leadership—an approach that connects concrete tasks to a common set of core values—allows employees to reach their utmost short- and long-term potential.

Of course, sometimes certain individuals are reaching their potential already; however, it usually isn't quite enough to move the tribe forward. In such cases, the right kind of leadership will uncover the reasons behind the inefficiencies by analyzing all four dimensions of a whole person: *knowledge* for the mind; *skills* for the body; *desire* for the heart; and *confidence* for the spirit. There is simply no way to improve employees with no knowledge, no desire, no skill, and no belief.

Conversely, some individuals may be completely passionate but not good at performing tasks. The response here is to find new roles for these people. Perhaps they are in the wrong seat on the bus, or on the wrong bus entirely. With a little hand holding, these folks can get back on track. But again, to know this for certain, the Z&C Leader must be able to diagnose that common core value set shared by these misplaced individuals as well as the organization.

Occasionally, employees ensnared in the concrete jungle will fight their Leaders' efforts off. Some will be naturally envious of their talents, while others will be embarrassed by their inability to achieve results on their own (or perhaps even in their previous roles as Leaders within the organization). It is absolutely crucial to establish a voice for both the tribe and the Leader from the very beginning. It must be part of the process before the Z&C Model is implemented, and it must start with the Leader finding his or her voice.

Voice of the Leader

In order for a Leaders to connect their core with things on the exterior, they—indeed, *you*—must find your voice before helping your tribe do the same (both individually and collectively). It's the same thing that occurs when parents constantly ask children what they want to be when they grow up; seldom do we adequately provide them with the steps to make that discovery themselves, the discovery of their personal, unique voice. Both of us found our voice early in life as coaches on the basketball floor. Coach Burt found it as the head coach at Woodbury Grammar. He would dress like former NBA coach Pat Riley and coach like him too. He considered his greatest achievement to be getting kicked out of an elementary school basketball game by challenging the calls of the officials.

Colby also found his voice early in life, signing on as an intramural coach at Saint Paul's Episcopal School in Mobile, Alabama, in the ninth grade. Colby personally coached his younger brother Zach, who was a point guard on a third- and fourth-grade team. Zach was a

77

decent player and was good at dribbling to his right rather than his left. The league had one rule and that was that all teams must play man-to-man defense. Knowing that, and knowing that kids follow directions in a literal way, Colby decided to try a new play.

He instructed his Zach to hold up the number one as he came down the court, and when the other members of the team saw that number they should run to their parents in the bleachers and give them a hug. Zach came down the floor, held up the number one, and the play was set into motion. The kids ran into the bleachers with defenders following. This left Zach one-on-one with his defender. He jabbed a step to the left and then lowered his head and went right and laid the ball in the basket. The plan didn't work. The game was stopped after the play and the point was waived. But it was at that point that Colby began to see how he could become a great coach by thinking differently.

We shortchange our followers similarly in a parallel discovery process; because we are their Leaders, they ask us the judicious question of how to facilitate this discovery. We therefore recommend using the following four probing questions to help them—and *you*—find a voice:

1. What are you *passionate* about?

     Passion is something that we all talk about. But do we really know what it means, and do we know how to apply it to our everyday lives? It's something you feel and something you live; something we have as kids but often lose somewhere along the way:

something that has meaning and virtue to us in and of itself—something we can clearly define. To find your passion, you must (re)discover it, feel it, and live it. But the only way to *feel* it is to first *define* it.

2. At what are you *naturally talented?*

Talent is something that exists inside of you and that you must somehow bring to the surface. It's both something with which we are born and something we develop, and it answers the question of why we exist. However, we sometimes shy away from our natural talents, due to the uncertainty associated with them. We might be afraid to hear someone say, "You can't make any money doing that" or "Exactly what are you going to do with that"? Therefore, the only way for you to discover your talents is by placing yourself in situations that force these talents to arise. Z&C Leaders allow and encourage this kind of discovery, because they support the notion that people can and should live through their passions and talents.

3. What does your *conscience* tell you?

The concept of conscience is related to meaning, purpose, contribution, and value. Z&C Leaders use conscience to filter the way they see the world, and to provide a view that answers even the most difficult questions. Becoming aware of these personal and organizational values allows the Leader to confront difficult decisions, instead of backing away from them.

4. Where is a *need in the world* that only you can fulfill?

This is the stage at which we connect our purpose to a need, thereby finding completion and fulfillment. It can be difficult and arduous to search for this need; as a result, many people, who fail to detect it rather quickly, give up trying to find it. These individuals usually need an encounter with another person to spark their search for this again. Z&C Leaders' task is therefore to look for that other person who can bring out the animal inside of them. Later in this book you will see how the Z&C Model is designed to help your people and organization determine these things by committing to a dominant aspiration with an emotional pull.

Voice of the Tribe

A Z&C Tribe exists because of the collective passion between the organization, its employees, and its customers. This kind of tribe is open to coaching and grounded in the entrepreneurial spirit, and it believes that its brand provides distinction, its management provides direction, and it has a differentiating advantage in the experience found within and then shared with others.

But before they can reach that point, the tribe must discover its voice by using a process very similar to that which the Leader uses. Tribes with a unified voice are able to carve their niches within the landscape of the concrete jungle.

In order to find that voice, you must ask your tribe the following four questions:

1. What is our tribe passionate about?

    Passion can be described as doing something each day for free and loving every minute of it.

2. How should our tribe define leadership?

    Leadership in the Z&C Model is as simple as "helping others find their unique voices," which you do by constantly discussing the questions found here.

3. How do we define successful execution as a tribe?

    This involves removing the gaps that exist between thinking about something to accomplish in the future, acting upon it, and making it happen.

4. How can our tribe design, establish, and perpetuate a culture that continually gives birth to our overall potential?

    Clearly, each tribe will do this in different ways. Some will use past failures to define what to avoid. Others will focus on the tribe's potential to create a necessary sense of collective passion.

The relationship between Leader and Tribe is the engine that drives the Z&C Model. Once we're aware that this engine is called *collective passion*, and that we must take tangible steps to create it, we develop a new focus on the relationship and how it should feel.

It Takes a Leader to Make a Tribe

We've mentioned previously that the concept of hand-holding that's often necessary during early stages of implementing this Model may sound a bit childish or un-needed. However, Dr. Stephen Covey, widely recognized as the one of the world's greatest thought Leaders and organizational expert, explained how practices that work with children would be equally successful with adults since, according to Covey, adults are nothing more than big children (something with which I'm sure many of us would agree). And Leaders operating in the concrete jungle will quickly realize that what people did as young adults defines much of what they do later in life.

After spending so many years as former coaches our-selves, working with high school and college students, we wondered if our material and methodologies would work with adults.

Although the process involves deeper dimensions and becomes far more complex when applied to adults, it remains comprised of essentially the same ideas that proved successful in building cultures that consistently won—embracing struggle, capitalizing on teachable mo-ments, seeing the forest and the trees, creating value from values, and defining dominant aspirations.

Struggle: The Key to Transferring Energy

Many people often lose sight of the value of struggle while building great Leaders and great tribes.

We should not view struggle as an end result, but rather a *path* meant to either help discover the voice we need or to help us decide that we should choose another path. In either case, we cannot find the correct path *without* struggle. It allows us to assess our environment and our tribe in new way. We match strengths to opportunities; we see weaknesses clearly and find ways to avoid or correct them; and we can ensure that the tribe and its members are doing things that give energy to the environment while simultaneously gaining energy from the work they're doing. And when the tribe makes a successful breakthrough, its energy is renewed and stored until the tribe can utilize and transfer it to the next struggle. Leaders make it clear that tribe members can derive greatness from overcoming obstacles, thereby teaching them to embrace struggles that lead to more successful breakthroughs.

Create a Scoreboard

Success comes from embracing the power that struggle can release. You can devise ways to gently but effectively harness power from difficulty, thereby creating mechanisms specifically designed to transfer the energy of struggle into tangible results.

One of the greatest ways to transfer this energy (which we discovered during our coaching careers) is through creating a scoreboard that motivates people to play harder in an effort to accurately measure and achieve defined outcomes.

A scoreboard represents the objective of the tribe's shared struggle, and allows individuals to clearly determine their progress in relation to the performance levels set for/ with them. You must design and carefully monitor this tool so that it does not create an environment of internal competition between tribe members. Such an approach will allow Culture the Gorilla to smash his way through the tribe again. The scoreboard's goal is instead to provide a way to translate struggle into efforts. If you want to see this idea in action, head out to any church league basketball game. Notice what happens when the scoreboards are turned on. The people playing the game become turned on too. The same people that sat next to each other in church praying together are now the people that, by virtue of the struggle (contest), increase their efforts in order to win!

Looking for Teachable Moments

Teachable moments foster the finding of some basic truths that lead people to better places over time.

With each new experience or educational endeavor comes new perspective and new understanding. You may have heard them called *teachable moments*. Teachable moments are born out of difficulty and struggle.

Though these kinds of teachable moments indeed include the moments themselves, they more importantly include the *reflection* that comes as a result of the experience. We listen to the truths we discover during those moments, and use them in the tribal planning process to bring about powerful change.

Teachable moments also generate questions that help us embrace something bigger than ourselves, and frequently allow us to gain insight from others' perspectives. Each one of these experiences imbues us with new waves of wisdom that give us the new mindset necessary to implement the Z&C Model. Further, these questions will help us discover what we know and, more importantly, what we *don't*.

However, Z&C Leaders realize that teachable moments can come about as byproducts derived only from the aforementioned process of struggle. In these cases, they can further be used to comfort their tribes during days of difficulty and encourage them to carefully watch and embrace what is unfolding.

Teachable moments happen with our children daily as they look to parents for understanding and often have question about what they are experiencing in life. It may happen in the grocery store when picking out foods that are healthy, a ball game when a player rises above others showing great effort, or at the park when learning how to play with others. But, teachable moments in business may be somewhat more difficult to see or act upon since adults, and all of their socialization, are now part of the equation. In the beginning of both of our careers, we would put together a concept, convince ourselves it would help others, and find anyone that we could pitch to.

After many failed attempts we finally encountered a teachable moment. We pitched to a property management company and thought we had closed the deal.

The following day we received word that they were not in a position to move forward with what we proposed. It was at that point that we both agreed it was time to define what our ideal client looked like. In that moment we learned that the audience you pitch to is just as important as what you are pitching.

In business, teachable moments are small windows of opportunities where you have to recognize what the adversity is trying to teach you at the moment.

Involvement: The Key to Teachable Moments

Leaders should develop teachable moments in ways that give each tribe member opportunities to become more involved. This involvement should unfold in a natural progression that begins with learning—specifically, about the tribe, its rituals, its history, the past challenges it's faced, and the successes and failures endured along the way. These lessons allow members to understand the tribe's story, and beckon them to join the tribe's pursuit of its ideals. This kind of engagement becomes the key to creating meaningful teachable moments.

Leaders must create an environment that encourages tribe members to share information. This is truly the only way they'll be able to build relationships and understand the role each member plays. This understanding can then create trust, and will allow each member to work better with others in the tribe. To aid this sharing process, it's crucial to designate a person within the tribe whose job is to speak to these things in a way that makes sense to each new tribe member.

Once you establish opportunities to learn, the focus can then turn to the question of how tribe members want to grow in their responsibilities. This means specifically that the tribe members are not evaluated annually for the sake of evaluation alone; they instead receive opportunities to explore new ways to add value to the tribe. As tribe members take on responsibilities, they will naturally tend to question how they can contribute to others' productivity. Each person will likely want to add to the good of the whole in his or her own distinctive way; this is certainly permissible, provided those contributions fit within the tribe's prescribed values.

The last step of involvement entails recognition of achievement. However, this recognition should be one of meaning, not another exercise of the Give-Each-Other-an-Award Society. Ask yourself when you recognize your tribe (individually or collectively): Why are you doing it? What exactly makes them deserve special recognition? How does it make them feel welcome in the tribe and reinforce the values that drive the tribe? Recognition with meaning is one of the most difficult things that Z&C Leaders must design as part of their creation of teachable moments, because recognition should be done in a way that lets the other tribe members know about the price that was paid and the process that was followed.

The point here is focusing on who deserves to be recognized and then doing it in a simple way. Review your system of recognition and ask yourself how difficult it is to recognize your people. How many steps does someone have to go through just to be considered for recognition? Higher education and other bureaucracies are notorious for stringent regulations in their reward process. Forms must be filled out, nominations made, and then colleagues vote, resulting in an adversarial, uncooperative environment.

Leaders are paid to make a decision. So do it. Stand up before your colleagues and say, "It's my job to recognize the people that are getting it done and this is what getting it done looks like. Every quarter we will gather and I will present awards to the people that we all know get it done."

See the Forest

The concrete jungle has many forests, made up of many trees. Leaders naturally find themselves having to decide whether their tribes should focus on the forest or the trees. With global challenges like time, technology, and transparency facing tribal members, seeing the forest requires a shift in focus away from seeing the trees, and it's something that members must do during formative, planning stages.

By seeing the big picture, tapping into the intensity of the tribe's values, and connecting to its members' core values, you will find that the view of the forest will provide a new level of focus, one that helps identify both internal and external trends and patterns. Exploration that uses questions, rather than simply pointing out problems, allows tribes to see the big picture in an entirely new way. It encourages an approach that starts a dialog during which the tribe can learn together, look at the terrain, and say collectively, *"This is what the forest is telling us."*

The questions could include:

- What things does the tribe consider to be most valuable?

- What broad issues may impact the tribe's future?

- What topics require our attention as we plan for the future?

See the Trees

In some cases, Leaders find themselves so close to something that they can't get a clear grasp of what is really happening. However, the point here is to pay attention to the little things.

You may find yourself overwhelmed with the challenges that lie ahead as a Z&C Leader; but staying focused on the small steps you can take will push the big concepts forward. As a concept, the Z&C Model requires doing these little things—or seeing the trees—first. However, you also have to take care that you aren't focusing *just* on the trees—that is, getting bogged down in the details. Ignoring the forest in this way may come as a result of being oversensitive to the concrete jungle. In these instances, you should review the overall Model as well as the action steps within it. This will help you see the trees and drive the larger concepts.

If you find yourself overanalyzing what your tribe is doing, remind yourself to check in with your intuition about how to implement the Model; this will keep the balance. The approach here is to not make the Model fit the people, but rather to make the people and the Model connect in order to see all of the possibilities.

Focusing solely on the trees—that is, becoming overly concerned with the small stuff—will cause the tribe to conclude that the very change to which they should be adapting is keeping the tribe from mastering the concrete jungle. It makes us question our expectations, our views of success, and the ability to remain as a coherent force in our current environment. The trees make us say, *All I need is patience, and this disruption (in this case, the implementation of the Model) and unpredictability will soon go away.* But remember: the Model must adjust to the tribe and its emotions. It must become a living part of the tribe. This is what maintains balance.

Remove the "S" from "Values" to Create Value

The heartbeat of the tribe is its core values; this is what comprises the collective passion that drives its actions and relationships. It is also the reason why people want to be a part of or spend time with your tribe.

When people ask you what your core values are, can you answer clearly and concisely? In his book *Good to Great*, Jim Collins suggests that core values are ideals that *under no circumstances* you would surrender. These are strong words; do they accurately project the importance of core values within the tribe? The concrete jungle is constantly shifting and evolving. This means that tribes must avoid adopting an all or nothing mindset. They must instead discern the reason why people do business with their tribe.

But can it be that simple? Could it be that all we need to do is remove the *s* from *values* to see the jungle in a new way? In this way, *values* become the foundation of the tribe as it relates to you, the decisions you make, how you choose to manage and lead, and ultimately, the legacy you will leave. *Values* define *value*—which means that we are able to connect our values to those outside our organization, thereby providing a foundation of the tribe's survival in the concrete jungle. Here are four reasons why:

1. Values determine the tribe's collective passion.
2. Collective passion drives actions.
3. Actions drive performance.
4. Performance ties directly to the explanation of who we are, what we do, and why we matter as an organization to those outside it.

Z&C Leaders must carefully monitor this cycle. It serves as a reliable barometer as to how well the core values of the tribe have been internalized and can be seen in its daily activities.

From Values to Dominant Aspiration

Leaders can develop a dominant aspiration by asking their tribes what they'd like to manifest within a given time frame. In real estate, this may be a certain number of homes sold, while in banking it might be a given number of new checking accounts established. Only one requirement accompanies its formulation: *It must be tied to a tangible outcome.* It should not be qualitative in nature with focus on things like "higher morale" or "better leadership." While those aspects are very important, their exact value varies by individual assessment or preference.

For instance, the dominant aspiration in athletics is to win. However, some coaches will say that 15 wins constitute a good season, while others claim that it takes 20 or even 25 wins. A coach who has not won 20 games may think that 10 wins makes a good season. Regardless, these numbers are quantifiable because, in any case, success is in the eye of the beholder and is constantly being (re)defined by the person who sets the goal and who is responsible for achieving it.

The same is true for companies; each employee possesses his or her own idea and definition of success. Therefore, energy must be harnessed in different directions in order to establish and reach a dominant aspiration. This is possible if the dominant aspiration ties into every employee's heart, mind, and conscience, and if Z&C Leaders are present to help create a shift that translates mindset into action.

A Coach-*What?*

Quoting Babylon, "Our actions are driven by our thoughts, and our thoughts are no wiser than our understandings." In other words, individuals cannot grow without learning to think smarter, perform better, and obtain a deeper understanding of both their occupations and their lives. We believe they need a person we call a *coachepreneur*. This is an individual who enters a business environment with the goal of improving employee performance, attitude, and overall being. Education is the key to our future, and a coachepreneur will educate an employee's mind, body, heart, and spirit, which will help create a transformation in the organization.

Coachepreneurs make this shift possible by placing employees in practice situations of artificial adversity that are aimed to prepare them for real-life adversity. These Leaders view individuals as whole beings comprised of multiple dimensions. They're capable not only of appealing to every single element within a person, but also of tapping into the deepest part of that person's nature in a way that will reveal his or her utmost potential.

People must perform in ways that they've never performed before, when they're attempting to achieve things that have never been achieved. Like athletic teams, businesses can easily find themselves running in place because of antiquated philosophies and industrial-age management practices that don't come close to reaching the deepest, most valuable elements of a person's nature: the mind, body, heart, and spirit. As we've previously noted, these four essentials are tied directly to an individual's performance in the workplace. At some point, mainstream thinking segregated the spiritual from the secular self. Life became compartmentalized, and work, home, and religion ended up in distinctly separate arenas. This outlook overlooked the fact that each component contributes to the creation of a wholly functioning and successful person. This is something that a coachepreneur recognizes, and why he seeks to ignite the kinetic energy within.

People often ask if individuals can be rewired to think in a different manner, and the answer is yes. Everyone is deeply scripted by genetics, just as everyone has been hardwired by culture, upbringing, and society. Additionally, everyone also reaches particular cognitive and maturity levels, at which point conscious decisions are made to change course. When we teach this concept of holistic thinking—four parts of nature with different needs and intentions that comprise one whole being—people become very alert and are eager to accept it. They realize that their spiritual lives are in fact not essentially separated from work, unless they choose to separate them. And even then, actual separation is impossible. This is why employees will often bring the stress of their home lives into their workplaces, and vice versa.

Aligning energies in one direction toward the notion of a *dominant aspiration* allows us to develop a better understanding of how the body, mind, heart, and spirit are intertwined. Z&C Leaders teach employees these concepts first and foremost. If one dimension is violated—if they don't show value toward the mind, or encourage growth—atrophy and complacency will develop. The mind is a muscle, and without exercise, it becomes weak. And the more flexing it undergoes, the sharper it will become. But without passion, an occupation is just a means to a financial end, one that is completely lacking in value and fulfillment.

A coachepreneur teaches the Model of the whole self and then finds ways to deepen it within the organization. They understand that bodies must be compensated fairly in order to live, to meet the financial realities of the world, and for nourishment. They're aware that minds need to be challenged, used creatively, and offered chances to grow; that hearts will swell from acknowledgment and appraisal of contributions; and that spirits require meaning and purposeful efforts.

Employees are free to choose how much of themselves to give, but they will not give themselves to careers they believe are going nowhere, nor to organizations with which they do not feel connections and fits—ones that stand out in the crowded concrete jungle with unique elements. And just like the relationship between Z&C Leaders and their tribes, this can only happen with intentional, deliberately creative efforts of a unique perspective, and then only by developing a unique mindset.

Tribe members will become passionate about the tribe and other members in it if they are provided opportunities to learn, chances to grow in responsibility, to contribute to others, and be recognized. Under each category, think about how you, as the Leader of your tribe, provide the following:

- Opportunities to learn
- Growth in responsibility
- Contributions to others
- Opportunity to be recognized

You and Your Tribe

Chapter 4

The 21st Century Compass: Creating a Dominant Focus

The Compass and Its Magnetic Pull

Imagine this: A person dressed a lot like you approaches you on a busy street. He or she grabs your hand, opens it, and puts a device resembling a timepiece face down in your palm. You flip it over and realize it's actually a compass. The person says, "Follow this, and you will connect with your dominant focus in life."

"My dominant *what*?" you say, utterly confused.

Most people are aware that a compass is a simple device consisting of a small, lightweight magnet balanced on almost frictionless pivot point. It obeys the natural laws that were true thousands of years ago, and will remain true thousands of years from today. As such, the compass remains a timeless symbol for the opportunity to choose the direction and the purpose to which we magnetically connect in life.

After looking a bit more closely, you notice a few strange things about the compass; it has no directional markings, and its needle is missing. It also has no signs for North, South, East, or West. Now you're a bit mystified.

You wonder, *Why did this person give this compass to me? After all, I'm not looking for directions.*

Hopefully, though, as a Z&C Leader, your thought process wouldn't end there. Instead, we'd like to think this kind of experience would bring you back to where you began to aspire to some special outcome for your life—the place where you first said, "I want to be in a better place than where I presently stand. I just need to figure out exactly *where* that is and *how* to get there."

Perhaps you started off in a particular direction that once seemed right to you. For a while, you felt like you'd made progress toward the place you'd envisioned; but today, you're not anywhere close to that place. This might have happened for one of several reasons. Perhaps you got close to where you'd originally wanted to be, only to discover that the grass there wasn't as green as you'd first believed. Perhaps rough, unanticipated environmental circumstances damaged your compass to the point of misdirection or uselessness; or maybe your compass brought you to cross rough terrain over which you weren't prepared or willing to travel. Or perhaps, in a fit of spontaneity, you elected to swap your old-fashioned compass for something more sophisticated that you thought would work better—something like a satellite-directed global positioning system (GPS), or the latest piece of technology you could find. So what does all this mean in terms of your career? In your twenties you hoped to graduate from college and find a job—any job. In your thirties you tried to climb within the organization you were working for. In your forties you tried to stay relevant within the organization.

Then, in your fifties you wake up and say, "What is it I really want to do with my life?" This can be a complex internal struggle. Greener grass should not be viewed as "greener" as compared to where you currently are. Greener grass is the place where you know what you wanted to do when you found your voice. It's the place that people wake up to in their fifties and finally admit to themselves: This is what I really want to do.

But why shouldn't I use a GPS instead of a compass, you reason. *Isn't a compass an old-fashioned piece of technology?*

Then you quickly rescue yourself by thinking, *How many times have I followed my GPS navigation system only to end up lost, or making the same u-turn multiple times before turning it off, looking for the sun, and taking it from there myself?*

So why do we need a compass instead of a GPS? Because the GPS has *no direct connection to us—and the compass does.* The GPS gets its signal from space, and this works most of the time. However, its signals can often be blocked by certain hindrances, such as changing conditions and unexpected obstacles. As a result, organizational direction—or original intentions—might be obscured or redirected. And you've surely seen the carcasses of many people and organizations that tried to make things too complicated by littering the concrete jungle. If we want to avoid such a fate, we need something to which we can directly attach and in which we can believe, even—in fact, *especially*—when the going gets rough.

Shaking your head, you realize that sometimes less is indeed more, and a simple compass might just be the more effective, efficient navigational tool for surviving in the concrete jungle. So ask yourself: To what can you connect in your organizational life that will remain as true and reliable as a compass? What can make us look different? Every one of us has something that fits this description, and we call this our *dominant focus*.

The Dominant Focus: An Organization's Compass

We've discussed dominant aspiration at several previous junctures as it sets the stage for the dominant focus of your tribe. Now we're about to share with you exactly how to discover and utilize the tool that will help formulate your unique perspective and unique mindset. Like a compass, a dominant focus is something that will directly connect your passion with a purpose and manifest itself by providing direction.

You must do the same thing on an organizational level to survive in the concrete jungle. That is, organizations must connect with a passionate purpose, and then formulate a structure that will allow them to fulfill that purpose. Notice that we said "a *passionate* purpose." This is important, because organizations that establish a dominant focus with an emotional pull will separate themselves from their competitors by deliberately and intentionally seeking change. In short, they'll *look* decidedly different. As with individuals, a dominant focus gives an organization a *shared* unique perspective, and it does a few other important things:

- **Transforms** an organization by painting a picture of what is possible.

- **Effectively aligns** an organization's people and purpose.

- Facilitates an organization's **planning**.

- Serves as a **catalyst** that moves an organization's agenda forward.

- **Releases stored energy**, but in a prescribed direction, not randomly.

- Is the **culmination** of the collective passion that exists between the organization and its employees.

But creating the dominant focus doesn't mean that we can just imagine a fictional, utopian Shangri-La, and then launch a blind, directionless voyage in pursuit of something that isn't real or attainable. The tribe must realize that they have to balance the dominant focus with the realities they face. Just as you wouldn't want to use a compass with no directional markings or needle, no one in an organization will be willing to blindly follow a management that's moving in an unclear, fantastic direction—at least, not for very long. They know that to struggle with no direction is more than just to be lost; it's also to be misunderstood.

Have you ever wondered exactly what some organizations have to offer, yet you can't quite figure it out, despite your best efforts? Some of you have done business with and/or worked for these companies. No one could accurately determine what those organizations actually *did*, either because it constantly changed, or because they tried to do so many different things in attempts to be all things to all people that they didn't do anything particularly well. Essentially, no one inside or outside those organizations could clearly focus upon them (yes, that's right . . . a *dominant* focus)—and this creates untold amounts of problems.

These companies lack a dominant focus. They don't have that thing that helps everyone in and around the tribe truly understand what it has to offer. It's also what gives them a chance to determine what steps they must take to further foster and act upon this understanding (because— say it with us—*they'll know how to look different!*).

A word of caution: discovering this dominant focus requires some deep soul-searching and reality wrestling. Tribe members must take measures throughout this process to identify the precise level of achievement they desire, and what provisions they need to attain it. Individuals need to determine what steps they're willing to take to expand their capacities. They also need to evaluate the price they're willing to pay to do so, not to mention the specific ways they need to equip, re-tool, or rewire themselves to get there.

Regardless of the extent of their expertise or career success, many (if not most) people who lead companies find themselves and their employees drastically under-equipped to advance at some point in their careers. They're in such a state that they cannot progress successfully, despite their best intentions. In other words, they starved to death in the concrete jungle. Yesterday's lunch won't drive away today's hunger, so people shouldn't expect old habits to automatically drive them to new heights of success when they're designing their dominant focus.

Starving in the jungle happens to everyone. Think about times when you had the greatest amount of growth in your life. When did that happen? Many of us will say it was in our high school or college days because we had a coach that pushed us to do more, to become more because we had so much more to give. We then age into our twenties and decide we will take on the world by ourselves. This is a bad idea.

Taking an independent approach to your professional career will hold you back by starving you of the relationships and networks needed to truly grow. Warning sign number one is not having a mentor. Do you have a mentor that understands who you are, where you are, and where you want to go? Warning sign number two is not having a coach. Just as you had great coaches and teachers who pushed you in high school and college, the same idea holds true in our adult professional lives. These are *not* the same people. A mentor is someone inside the organization that listens to you while providing an honest dialogue about the role you play in the organization now and the one you want to pay in the future. A coach teaches you new skills, challenges you to become more by making you face the mistakes you made in the past, and adopting new skills sets for the future. Coaches tell you the truth no matter what the cost.

Though obviously painful and complex, the struggle to determine your purpose in an organization will allow you to develop values that lead to your organization's dominant focus. And you don't begin this process by asking outright, *"What should our organization's core values be?"*

Instead, values should be assimilated as a response to the call of the concrete jungle. Once tribe members have clearly heard that call, they can begin to answer the following three questions, which will help connect them to a workable set of core values.

1. Why are tribe members doing what they are doing?
2. Why/how does the work of each tribe member matter, and how does it serve the tribe?
3. How can tribe members work together with collective passion?

Chances are, the tribe will debate and struggle with this matter for a while. However, when everyone involved understands the power of this idea, a new level of growth can begin to take place, and *they'll begin to look different.* And when you get to this point, you know the organization is ready to develop a unique perspective.

But before we discuss that concept in detail, let's go back to the scenario of you and the compass with no labels.

I've always enjoyed the "re-creation" period that takes place at the end of each season of my coaching career. This happened while transitioning from one experience or season to the next. I usually took several months to create themes that tied into the team's specific phases. I used various works such as *Good to Great* or *Become a Category of One*, *Become the Power of Attention*, or *From Effectiveness to Greatness*. We ate, slept, and internalized these ideas as a team. Each theme became our culture, our mantra, and the driving force behind the personality that the team would eventually develop. Each team required a fresh unique perspective, and each season required a unique mindset, because the challenges were always different. Some teams were underdogs who needed to prove that they could compete; others were favorites who needed to deal with the high expectations heaped upon them.

Upon dissecting these works and their themes, we decided at the beginning of each season that good was not good enough. Every teammate pledged her solidarity to the chosen theme. I told every player, "If you don't want to go there, then don't tell me you want to go there." Then we discussed—as opposed to me telling them—what attributes a great team possesses. I asked them where they wanted to go during that season. My job as their coach was to get them to where they wanted to be, which meant I had to hold them accountable. I had to push when the

(continued)

The 21st Century Compass: Creating a Dominant Focus

(Continued)

team wasn't achieving the level of performance needed. I was their biggest supporter and loudest cheerleader.

Aside from all the winning we were able to do, the greatest thing about managing these teams was the fact that I was only helping them do the things that *they* told me they wanted to achieve. They chose their ambitions themselves; these goals were not anything I had somehow forced upon them. The power of collective passion drove the team to win after win; using this Model, all I soon had to do was simply serve as a (sometimes friendly, sometimes not-so-friendly) reminder of what they had chosen to do. But had we not painstakingly devoted time to developing a unique perspective and unique mindset each season, the program would never have come remotely close to achieving the levels of greatness it came to regularly enjoy.

—*Coach Burt*

Labeling the Compass: Creating a Unique Perspective

A few minutes after you realize the importance of a compass, a second person approaches you with four labels for your directionless, needleless compass. But the labels, like the face of the compass, are blank as well. This person instructs you to place them on the compass only *after* you write on them the four things that you would utilize to direct your life.

A compass provides the magnetic pull that launches your journey. But utilizing that pull to choose what direction to pursue always comes from the choices you make. So in order for your compass to guide your dominant focus, you must decide which directional labels you will place on each of the compass's signs. Said in a way that's more familiar to you by now: confidently knowing the direction in which you're going can allow you to run much, much faster!

So ask yourself—if you were given this blank compass today, what would you write on those labels? What factors have provided direction for you in your personal and professional endeavors? Regardless of whether you realize it, the labels will be placed on the compass by you or someone else. It's your compass. Shouldn't you decide?

Let's look at this way. If someone said to you, "Tell me about yourself, but start at the beginning," how would you respond?

How about starting with something like, "My life focus begins with _____."

Wouldn't that help provide some perspective about you for someone else?

Here's another: "The course of my life was changed because of _____."

Or maybe: "The course of my life will never change because of _____."

Then perhaps: "When my life ends, the one thing for which I most want to be remembered is _____."

What words would you use to describe the things that have steered you to this point? Would they be words like *Family*, *Fear*, *Faith*, or *Fortune*? Would they be more tangible words—a title to which you've aspired, a milestone that you would like to achieve, or an age to which you would like to live? We find ourselves asking so frequently in both life and work. "How did I end up here"? We can usually answer this question by tracing the steps back to the point of where the journey began.

So take a step back now and reflect upon where *you* began to gain the perspective you currently have. Some people will revisit the painful days of a first job—certainly a natural place for many individuals to begin. Others will focus on one or two outstanding moments of serendipity or crisis that have brought them to their current places. Some people have experienced a series of related moments that cause to see the world in a certain way. Still others may not be able to pinpoint any specific factors at all. They just got in the rat race with intentions of making a living, and somehow were pushed, pulled, and punted into career situations they now despise.

Interestingly, each of these different situations has at least one thing in common: Whether they realized it or not, these people have been shaped and defined by their *values*, and they've acquired these as a result of their various experiences.

But what about the people who "just want to make a living," or are "just trying to get by," or "can't help it if life turned me that way"? Were they just victims of circumstance? As calloused as it may sound, no.

These individuals either adopted a set of values that didn't work well (by leading them in a counterproductive direction); or they adopted others' values without truly examining whether they fit their personal parameters. Generation Y Leaders in particular need to understand this concept, because they too often spend time seeking guarantees rather than searching for ways to take smart risks and excel. As a result, they're running, but not as fast as they could be if they had direction. They soon find themselves entrenched in old-school management philosophies asking, "What's in it for me"? Instead, they should ask, "How can my unique perspective be added to this equation?" Mahatma Gandhi established this idea in fewer words, stating, "No wealth can be gained without work, and no pleasure can be experienced without conscience." The second part of his thought is what is important to the matter at hand. Our conscience tells us what directions to pursue, and we must listen, even in the workplace.

This is a very simple but important principle used to reinforce the notion that people manifest those things *to which they pay attention*. If you're uncertain of your direction, you have almost no chance of finding success. That may be tough to accept—but think just for a moment. Chances are you can identify at least a handful of individuals you know who were consumed by a pit in the concrete jungle—something they never saw coming until it was too late. How does this happen? Let's examine that question by looking at the difference between performance, production, and profits.

The 21st Century Compass: Creating a Dominant Focus

The Pits of Performance, Production, and Profits

During recent years, emerging patterns of disconnect between workable core values and organizations have increasingly emerged. Asking a general question like, "As an employee, to what do you connect within your organization?" provides a glimpse of the real challenges Leaders face. Why? Nine times in 10, responses will be tied to some concrete outcome that usually revolves around a performance measure. If the answer isn't tied to individual performance, then it will probably be tied to production. If neither of these, then it's probably focused on profits. In each case, such answers focus on *outcomes*—not *ideas* that could be universally and perpetually driven through the individuals and the organization.

It's even more telling when individuals state that the organization for which they currently work has no clear values to which they can connect. This subsequently forces them to question *why* they got into their profession or went to work for that organization in the first place. If the lack of values isn't the case, they'll often identify a severe disconnect between what values they state and behaviors they continue; or they might claim that the organization operates according to a set of dated/weak/irrelevant values. Here is what alignment means – you love what you do, you love who you do it with, and its based on a set of shared values. Think about any great relationship you have had with another person. What

was it based on? Certainly one of those is shared values.
Ask yourself:

Do I love what I do?

Do I love who I do it with?

Do we have a set of shared values?

Regardless of the specific nature, these kinds of values crises perpetuate wear and tear on the people within organizations where the crises exist; accordingly, those people begin to focus on the shortsighted things they can control (or *think* they can control). Yes, outcomes are important; but they're only means to an end and should *never* be the dominant focus, because they don't provide consistent direction. And without this, it's impossible to run faster.

A clear example of this comes from a conversation we had with a veteran athletic administrator. Upon suggesting that he establish a set of core values for his athletic department (and provided outline of the process, as well as associated benefits and challenges), he quickly balked: "I think you're making this too complicated. We're just trying to win games and graduate kids around here."

Anyone who knows anything at all about the convoluted, multilayered concrete jungle environment of intercollegiate athletics knows that it's just not that simple As the complexities of this arena continue to spiral out of control, isn't *now* the time to implement a solid organizational platform? Establishing core values would allow an athletic department's various stakeholders (coaches, athletic administrators, school administrators, student-athletes, faculty, donors, and fans) to have clear directions to follow. It would also show how their collective passion could then act as a magnet that unilaterally and *quickly* pulls all groups in the organization's singular direction,exactly as a compass would do. They'd be able to avoid their individual pitfalls that come when they make performance, production, and/or profits their dominant focus.

You might be thinking, "Well, a good personnel housecleaning would probably take care of a stagnant organization like that athletic department." But even if that were possible (and as with most facets of higher education, it's almost impossible), that alone wouldn't work. Just as within many organizations like it, the actual challenge in this situation (beyond attracting the right people) is to align personnel with a specific purpose. But in order to do that, the organization must begin with a values-driven dominant focus, and then link that to a unique perspective. Otherwise, its members are trying to utilize a label-less compass, and they can't do anything *quickly* because they have to think through everything they do from the ground up before acting. Once labeled, the compass allows you to gain perspective, provides a point of reference as you pursue your dominant focus, and positions you to move toward it with *agility*! Succinctly, we call that a *unique mindset*.

Ready for Action: The Unique Mindset

Let's go back one last time to your now-not-quite-so-mysterious compass. Though it's much closer to being functional now that you've labeled it, it's still not quite ready for use. Although you know how important a tool it is, and although its directive benchmarks are now in place, you still have no needle to point you toward a specific course of action while dodging any expected or unexpected obstacles you encounter in the concrete jungle.

As if on cue, a third stranger appears. He gives you the delicate last piece to your compass (the needle), and says, "Attach this unique mindset to your unique perspective in order to find your way."

We built the Z&C Model—to which you'll be introduced in the next chapter—upon the understanding that people must share the same perspective. This is the foundation that translates to mindset, which then leads to action. We've already talked about running in the concrete jungle, but you had better know two things before you start running: what you're running from, and what you're running toward. Motives that are constantly impacted by internal and external forces become muddled with change for the sake of change. Therefore, clear pathways to success become less transparent if the unique perspective and unique mindset aren't adequately in place throughout the organization.

Consequently, all directives become hollow company rhetoric and noisy cognitive dissonance, which makes it increasingly difficult to find any kind of fulfillment. In other words, people lose *agility*. Exasperated employees then grumble quietly to themselves (if not aloud to superiors), "What does any of this really *mean*"? What should have been a point of unification becomes a catalyst for frustration. However, this frustration didn't manifest through just one act, which means that it can't be undone with just one act, either. You can accomplish a shift in mindset, however, through a carefully designed process. We call this "The Shift"—and it begins by drawing a line in the sand.

To be agile, you've got to cultivate a mindset of *see the need, fill the need*. In other words, Z&C Leaders see opportunity when other don't want to or simply can't.

Remember, three assumptions must be met before a tribe can become agile and experience true change.

To persevere through the concrete jungle:

1. The tribe must be made up of the right people.

2. The tribe has a genuine desire to make a shift in the concrete jungle.

3. The tribe has the capacity to make that shift in one of these areas: knowledge, skills, desire, confidence, likability, and networks.

How do you know if you're agile?

It starts with a unique thought process in the mind of the entrepreneur, CEO, or founders of a company. It's a mindset that says that opportunity is abundant and infinite, and it means taking a step when others will stop at only wondering, "What if . . . ?" Early on in our career, Colby and I took meetings with the wrong people, wasted time on opportunities that would seldom materialize, and generally fished in the wrong ponds. We began to ask ourselves how could we create something of such great value that other people would want to buy it, rather than us simply selling it.

To do this, we first had to identify characteristics of what we thought the ideal client would look like. These four characteristics defined who we wanted to work with and represented the ideals of Z&C Leaders found in this book.

They are:

1. Enlightened people who are open to making shifts in their businesses and lives.

2. Unique perspectives that cause them to look at their businesses differently.

3. Vested partnerships where both parties have "skin in the game" and will do what is required to find the success we mutually seek.

4. This results in collective passion or meaningful relationships created between the customer, organization, and employee.

A great example of Z&C Leaders are Shane Reeves and Rick Sain, owners and CEOs of a $40 million suite of medical services. Reeves-Sain represent the best of these characteristics.

With seven divisions and revenue streams flowing from each, what started as a local pharmacy is now growing into a national personalized, specialized medicine company.

Since both owners were enlightened to the idea of coaching and possessing an entrepreneurial core, they saw a need and brought to market personalized, specialized products and services that customers wanted.

A Line in the Sand

As you know by now, Z&C Leaders look different, run faster, and are more agile than those around them. With unique perspectives of entrepreneurs and unique mindsets of coaches, they spring into action and work at a pace that allows them to act with speed, precision, and conviction—all while maintaining full commitment to the Model's implementation (i.e., *agility*).

Armed with a dominant focus and a unique perspective, Z&C Leaders will establish an agile mindset by drawing a line in the sand. This essentially says that past practices will no longer suffice, and that they're defining a new level of productivity within the organization. They now expect r*esults*.

Naturally, not all employees will receive this kind of announcement well. It will often be followed by a fall-out period during which some tribe members will decide they don't want to participate in the shift that is taking place. This period will clearly show Leaders which employees should be part of the tribe and which should be asked to leave.

We should note that it's not always possible to discover this distinction in agility isn't in the beginning. Rather, it's is often revealed in the end. It will become more apparent as focus and pressure grow, and tribe members are asked to increase production. This process will naturally eliminate those individuals who prefer not to make The Shift from mediocrity to new levels of purpose with the rest of the tribe. And truly, the tribe is better off without those who aren't willing to take this journey.

It will take some time to transform from an average tribe to a great one. However, you cannot begin the process until the line in the sand is drawn. Agility therefore begins with a refusal to revert to old ways.

Communicating the Content of The Shift

In order to achieve success, Z&C Leaders must believe that all things are possible. They must be willing to break with the old ways, and adopt new methods of learning by remaining humble and coachable.

The truth is that the natural human reaction is to resist any time change from taking place. Many people who face uncertainty want to focus on how the organization has morphed into something that they don't like or won't accept, which only highlights how crucial it is to establish a values-driven unique perspective. Given this tendency to fight change, how can current and future tribe members begin to make The Shift in their own lives *and* in the tribe? It begins with effectively communicating how to take the steps that allow The Shift to take place.

Z&C Leaders are responsible for bringing a sense of practicality and reality to the purposeful change that's at the forefront as the tribe readies to make The Shift.

This is truly an example of agility at its finest. Furthermore, they understand that tribe members want to know two pieces of information more than anything else—and it's not how much they're going to be paid, or how many off days they'll have. They simply want to know what their future will look like under your leadership, and what their future with the tribe will look like. This is the first phase of preparing to communicate the content of The Shift.

The next step is to *remove distractions*, another key point in perpetuating agility. One of the biggest concerns for tribe members is the question of whether they will be permitted to freely express their viewpoints. They'll also wonder whether their Leaders will actually take those viewpoints *into consideration* as they become more comfortable with The Shift.

You can ease your tribe's worries by assuring them that they have permission to find that place of comfort in *their own ways*. Let them also know that you'd actually prefer to do more listening than talking during The Shift. It's crucial that Leaders put themselves in the position of other tribe members to truly understand their points of view. Listening must become focused during this time; you want to not just accept but encourage questions from the tribe concerning The Shift. This outlook leads to better understanding of The Shift and the roles each tribe member will play during it, and thereby creating greater agility.

Each member will internalize The Shift in different ways, and it can then begin when tribe members become humble and teachable. This final step in preparing to communicate The Shift is absolutely critical, because it can't and won't happen until the tribe can get to this place. Z&C Leaders should look for cues from tribe members to see how close they are to finding this place in their personal and professional lives.

Once they're open and eager to learn, you can communicate the content of The Shift by taking the following five steps:

1. **Get to a place where you and others are *able to make* The Shift *happen*.**

   You'll need knowledge, training, experience, and equipment to make The Shift happen. Does your tribe have these things? Are they where they have to be, and equipped to create the needed changes?

2. **Begin to internalize The Shift *by living it*.**

   The more the tribe discusses The Shift, the more meaning it will have to them, and the better they will understand it. This is a very simple but powerful piece of the puzzle.

3. **Strengthen The Shift *by teaching it to others*.**

   Inevitably, each tribe will contain stragglers who are slow to adopt The Shift. These people will likely respond much more favorably to effective messages about The Shift from peers than through managers, so having a team of "Shift emissaries" is an important factor in successfully executing this transformation.

The 21st Century Compass: Creating a Dominant Focus

4. **Package The Shift in a way _the world understands_.**

Teaching The Shift to peers is also a great way to prepare the tribe to teach it to those outside the organization. Your tribe will need to educate its constituents about The Shift before all can truly benefit from it.

5. **Make The Shift _scalable_.**

Rome wasn't built in a day; and neither were Chick-fil-A, Apple, or Walmart. While there's no denying the shifts these organizations created, they were once acorns that eventually became mighty oaks. Z&C Leaders must similarly encourage employees to individually change a little bit every day until The Shift becomes a larger collective one with landscape-changing results.

Here's a typical story we have heard often about overcoming dysfunction.

A superior hired a consultant to lead a workshop that would supposedly help a department "overcome its dysfunction." After hours of discussion that seemed like a days-long death, the consultant's answer was to have the department create what Jim Collins and Jerry Porras called "BHAG" in their 1996 book _Built to Last_. "BHAG" is an acronym for "Big Hairy Audacious Goals," and the consultant seemed convinced that creating lofty, far-reaching aims would suddenly motivate the former anemically-producing department.

Everyone seemed to support this notion after the consultant preached from Collins and Porras gospel— everyone, that is, but Bill. After a show of hands affirmed the BHAG buy-in, the consultant singled out Bill and asked why he hadn't raised his hand.

Bill replied, "I sincerely appreciate your insight into the work of Collins and Porras, because I'm a big fan of their work, which I, too, have read and absorbed, including the Hedgehog Concept."

The Hedgehog Concept, first discussed in Collins' landmark work *Good To Great*, consists of a Venn diagram with three overlapping circles that represent:

- What are we passionate about?
- What can we be the best in the world at doing?
- What drives our economic engine?

Bill continued his response to the consultant: "My simple question to you is this: how can we set big, hairy, audacious goals and expect to achieve them when we don't know what we're passionate about, what we can be the best in the world at doing, or what drives our economic engine?"

You could have heard a pin drop! The consultant had nothing to say in response, and from that day forward, Bill began to have a new perspective about the organization and where it wanted to go.

Here is the point: goal-setting should happen only after much bigger concepts are firmly set in place, or they won't amount to much. Does your tribe have a Bill? If not, they need one.

—*Colby Jubenville*

Connecting Mindset to Action

Another move towards agility requires that Z&C Leaders let everyone know that mediocrity will not be subsidized. They will no longer consider things like past performances or typical excuses valid. They'll no longer tolerate the need to inform individuals of their responsibilities, or won't put up with people who simply acknowledge that available self-improvement tools exist but fail to utilize them.

The sad fact is that most companies operate in a culture where management's mindset focuses on the bottom line—rather than the tribe's emotional needs or desires. While employees must indeed produce enough revenue to fund salaries, the dominant focus must also include something *emotionally* attractive; otherwise, the tribe won't entirely invest in the cause.

So exactly how can Z&C Leaders establish plans of action that are at once measurable, manageable, and meaningful? The key to changing behavior and creating action is to appeal to all aspects of a person including body, mind, heart, and spirit.

There Is an "I" in "Incentivize"

Goals are one of the most misused and abused concepts in business and life today. Quite often, they're set but not met, or set without providing realistic aims and/or equipment to achieve them. As a result, goal outcomes are often lowered until they are met, or scrapped entirely in favor of new ones. Sometimes people will meet new ones, and sometimes not; and the fruitless goal cycle begins anew. But the question still remains: *After all this goal-setting, where did we really end up?* We probably don't know, because we're exhausted from trying to hit moving targets!

Yet despite this typically reckless use of goals, Z&C Leaders should attempt to build programs with aims that incentivize their entire organizations once they've established The Shift. This will prove difficult, and it usually becomes more so the larger an organization is or becomes. We all know that it's nearly impossible to create programs that appeal to each individual. This is why Leaders must understand how to develop incentive plans tied to and that can engage all four parts of a person's nature that we first cited in Chapter 2: the *body*, the *mind*, the *heart*, and the *spirit*.

The *body's* need is to live; financial means provide for that need. This is clearly why incentive plans must have a financial component, so that when members of the tribe make money for the organization, individuals make money for themselves, too. The *mind's* need is to learn; therefore, incentive plans must also incorporate regular, systematic, comprehensive growth programs. Organizations need their associates to improve, but they often fail to supply the tools necessary for such advancement (this is precisely why the concept of hiring coaches in the business world will become increasingly popular: top management is realizing that coaches can grow, train and lead employees).

The 21st Century Compass: Creating a Dominant Focus

But in addition to the financial and mental attractiveness that so many companies provide, the incentive plan must also tap into the heart and spirit of people, something many organizations sadly miss. Because the *heart's* need is to be valued and appreciated, tribes must value, recognize, and promote individual contributions among the entire tribe. You have to create various mechanisms that constantly celebrate individual and collective success: not the mundane success like sustained respiration, but *real* success that actually matters (what is "success that actually matters"? *Anything that drives the organization forward toward its dominant focus!*).

For example, we worked with Fayetteville, North Carolina, based H&H Homes. Ralph and Linda Huff, the owners and founders, were two people that built the company from humble beginnings up to selling 350-plus homes a year. In 2009, they experienced a slip in sales (like most home builders that year) and decided to engage us to bring a dominant focus to the company.

Together we came up with a race-themed employee dominant focus to sell 450 homes over the course of 12 months; it was dubbed the H&H 450. Over 12 months the company rewarded employees with spa treatments, regional vacation packages, and a grand prize trip to New Orleans on Ralph's private jet. Ralph dressed up in a racecar uniform and called himself Racin' Ralph in meetings and to employees on job sites. The company rented out a local theater to show *Talladega Nights and Days of Thunder*. Throughout this process H&H employees were more engaged and sales and spirits increased.

Ultimately, the *spirit's* need is to leave a legacy, to matter, and to contribute. To satisfy this component, company Leaders must enmesh personal and company visions and ask how members of the tribe want to become involved in enhancing their community.

Believe, Belong, Become

If time and energy are the two most valuable assets a person can possess, then people must take action in a planned direction daily. Numerous high-value activities, from phone calls to follow-up e-mails, can move individuals and companies closer to success. It's easy to maintain focus when you combine specific actions with a dominant focus; and Z&C Leaders will build these types of systematic programs into their tribes.

Effective communication is critical to achieve these accomplishments; members can be easily sidetracked from the main focus, either because they are unaware of it, or because they are unsure of their specific role. Leaders must continuously communicate with tribe members to ensure that they're aware of accountability. Accordingly, members must fully understand how the overall focus is tied directly to their performances, which are thereby tied directly to their roles within the tribe.

Z&C Leaders must understand that they promote what they permit. Therefore, certain things must remain nonnegotiable; and if an organization is going act upon its dominant focus, find direction with its unique perspective, and chart a course for action with its unique mindset, tribe members need to either get on board or get out of the way. The tribe has spoken; the line in the sand has been drawn; and movement toward the differentiating dominant focus has begun in a speedy, agile manner.

And if you'll turn the page, you will take your first step toward using your newly completed compass by learning the Z&C Model that will help unlock the dominant focus of your tribe.

Developing a dominant focus begins with labeling your compass. If you were going to write the labels on your compass, what would they be?

What is the dominant focus for you or your tribe?

A dominant focus is realized through a shift in the way your tribe thinks, acts, and responds. Use the following questions to identify The Shift that must take place in your tribe.

1. What is the message?
2. How can you internalize or live the message?
3. How can you teach the message to others?
4. How can you package the message to others?
5. How can you make the shift scalable?

Chapter 5

The Zebras and Cheetahs Model: Making Growth Simple, Engaging, and Fun

Now that you are equipped with a compass, guided by unique perspective and mindset, and driven by a dominant focus, you are able to take on the concrete jungle's challenging landscape.

But having the compass only acts as a guide. It's not time to spring into action! To ultimately become a Z&C Leader, you must first shape public perception by leveraging the channels around you to successfully highlight your unique perspective, education, experience, and qualities. You must become more than the person carrying the compass; you must also use it to devise a map that persuades and allows others to follow you through the concrete jungle. In essence, you must become a person that others have heard about and need to know.

In this chapter, we turn you into a concrete cartographer—that is, we teach you how to use the Z&C Model and the compass to create a map that will effectively lead your tribe in the concrete jungle. We give you five simple yet effective map-making tools that are simplistic and effective to create the Model. But before we do, let's introduce some concepts that will help you become a good mapmaker.

Shine Bright like the Sun

Most people know of Nicolaus Copernicus (1473–1543), the Renaissance-era astronomer who first proposed that the Sun, *not* the Earth, was the center of the universe. His book, *On the Revolutions of the Celestial Spheres,* is considered the foundation of modern astronomy and the defining moment of the scientific revolution. Initially, however, Copernicus's work was subjected to a great deal of criticism from the astronomic, philosophic, and religious communities. Yet his idea and its eventual flurry of acceptance provide two outstanding lessons for Z&C Leaders.

First, any time you shake up conventional methodology, you better know whereof you speak, because you are certainly going to be grilled about it. We've already prepped you for that with previous discussions, but we need to reinforce it once again at this juncture. This is when you're on the cusp of moving the tribe into the throes of the battle, and when that movement occurs, you'll need every underpinning you can get.

Second, you must find a way to create a new "center of the universe." This means making the concrete jungle revolve around your organization and its position, which is the key to being recognized in this environment. And while it might sound simple, it's not so easy to do. Your tribe must become something innovative, different from the norm, and memorable, and then find ways to tell your story in ways that people can easily comprehend.

So how do you shape the perception you want others to have of you? In addition to possessing the foundation of knowledge, you must present yourself as an expert in the way you speak and dress, what you reference, and how you reference it. The tribes seated before you must hear and believe what you say in a way that resonates with them before they will go and get results.

We cannot overemphasize this concept's critical importance; the manner in which you present your dominant focus is crucial to shaping perception along two fronts. The more easily identified is what we call the *front-stage sale*, which must persuade people outside your organization to want your product, do business with your company, utilize your services, and so on. But equally—and perhaps *more*—important is the *back-stage sale*, which is where you create buy-in to the team *inside* the organization.

Back-stage sales are every bit as critical as front-stage sales; however, they're not happening as they should be as far as we can tell. We learned while coaching how absolutely necessary it is to sell to people *inside* the locker room before we could expect anyone *outside* the locker room. We knew we would be held responsible regardless of whether we were successful or not, but one thing was for certain: we wouldn't get positive results if we couldn't put together a map (or Model) toward a successful future with a dominant focus in which players could first place their faith.

Over the years of coaching, and later as coaches of present and future Leaders, we began to assemble tools with which this could be accomplished. Before we detail them, here's a quick glance at the list of five tools.

1. Equip with focus and emotion.

2. Empower with excellence.

3. Create the scoreboard.

4. Coach 'em up.

5. Throw in thunderbolts.

Because the science of cartography (mapmaking) is largely mathematical, we decided each tool should have its own mathematical equation to further illustrate how to use it. As we go forward, we'll break down each tool and formula. But don't worry; we only went as far as to add two things together to equal a third, so if you can comprehend $1 + 2 = 3$, you'll be in good shape!

1. Equip with Focus and Emotion

Equation: Dominant Focus + Emotional Pull = Staying Power

American philosopher/poet/writer Ralph Waldo Emerson once wrote, "Nothing great was ever achieved without enthusiasm."

While that quote's worth is fairly self-evident—and while we embrace it wholeheartedly—what it doesn't tell you is *why* that happens; or how to help spawn that enthusiasm, first within yourself, and then within others. That's where the contents of this book can help, both in our previous discussion of the dominant focus and in this chapter's subsequent discussion. We analyzed the dominant focus in the previous chapter, and while it's certainly a cornerstone concept for Leaders to master, it does little good by itself. Now we're about to make it more useful by sharing how to use it to put the Z&C Model into motion.

Let's begin by giving you some examples of other books that have a well-stated dominant focus, Take a look at the following statements (and read the books when you get a chance), and see if you can pinpoint a common quality among them:

- *Going from Good to Great* (book by Jim Collins)
- *Becoming a Category of One* (book by Joe Calloway)
- *Using the Power of Intention* (book by Wayne Dyer)
- Becoming a rock star or Z&C Leader in your industry. (This is *your book*!)

You probably noticed fairly quickly that most (if not all) of the statements elicit some sort of gut reaction within you. After all, can't we easily see that the condition of "great" is better than the condition of "good"—and ask yourself this: If you had a chance to be great, would you seize that over just being good? What if you were truly someone about whom others said, "I just can't compare

131

The Zebras and Cheetahs Model

him or her to anyone else. By virtue of what he does and how he does it—he is just so different." Hanging out in the concrete jungle like a fish that actually lives out of water (and likes it)!

Can't most of us understand the desire to have ownership of something? Haven't we all been touched by the power of realization at some point in our lives? Doesn't almost everyone have at least a measure of a desire to be a rock star somewhere inside (for evidence, look no further than the video games *Guitar Hero* and *Rock Band*—as well as the global popularity of karaoke)?

Your gut reactions to those statements were based on *emotional connections* you have something to which you relate—dominance, greatness, oneness, intention, being a rock star. And because you connect with them in this way, you could envision yourself proceeding forward, which is exactly what a dominant focus should equip you to do. After all, a dominant focus is a conceptual idea that you can use to build a theme into the organization's fabric, and drive home through unique activation points.

The lack of a dominant focus is what causes so many modern organizations' strategic efforts, well intended though they may be, to go awry. This includes the age-old practice of goal-setting, which we touched on in the previous chapter, and which we'll discuss in greater detail in the next section of this one. While we understand the power of goal-setting, this process is simply hollow in far too many cases. It's easy to state some desired outcome and call it a goal; but how can you expect to take action upon it without an emotional pull? And even if you do act in some way, how can a manager count on that action being sustained over time? Furthermore, does the goal even make sense, and how does someone *know* that it makes sense? These kinds of questions show us where the foundation of a dominant focus *really* comes into play.

There is a saying that "not all dreamers are achievers, but all achievers are dreamers." We can apply this incredibly accurate statement to companies as well as individuals, particularly to Z&C Leaders, who have the ability to create game plans based upon dominant focuses that have the ability to harness employees' energies. This occurs when the dominant focus makes such a strong emotional connection that it forces people to imagine a dream so compelling, so wonderful, and so adventurous that it keeps them up at night, wakes them up in the morning, and constantly lingers on their minds. The scenes they subsequently create in their minds are visualizations of things that have not yet manifested but that nevertheless have magical pull.

Something magical happens when things snowball to that point: *The dominant focus becomes a component of the essence of the tribe.* They are both inspired—meaning literally, *to breathe life into*—and motivated (which means *to move*). Every memo, every meeting, every e-mail, every seminar . . . *everything* is then created around a theme.

Consider this concept using the rock star motif:

- You plan a training seminar for salespeople who've completed their first year, entitled "How to Go from a One-Hit Wonder to a Legend."

- You assemble an operations training manual entitled "What Should Be Done Backstage to Have a Great Front Stage."

- You compose a company newsletter article on generating subsequent sales, entitled "Groupies: How to Be a Rock Star Salesperson with a Following."

If you're trying to grasp the idea of a dominant focus more concretely, think of a sports team that wins a national championship. The achievement of becoming the best within a given group of talented competitors is the single greatest reason that any game is played. Too often within companies, however, people don't know what the dominant focus for any given period of time really *is*, which means that they have no idea how their specific roles are tied to it, or what's in it for them. Imagine how lost a sports team with no championship objective would be. If that seems to be an absurd scenario for people playing games, imagine how absurd it must be for organizations upon which people depend to earn their very livings!

Throughout my coaching career, I worked diligently to avoid having a team with a scattered mindset. I did this by doing everything possible to identify, develop, and reinforce our team's dominant focus for that season. It was the topic of every meeting, discussion, and initiative that took place. All team members clearly knew both our focus and their exact roles in helping us achieve the dream for that season. We also created a well-defined incentive system, designed to boost members within their roles by rewarding them for completing activities that propelled the team toward its dominant focus. All incentive plans spoke to the whole person, inspiring the players in each dimension of the performance sectors needed to achieve our dominant focus (in parentheses, you'll see some real-world organizational equivalents, though most are universally translated from teams to organizations): body (financial), mind (learning and growth), heart (success and validation), and spirit (meaning and legacy).

Winning a championship as a former high school girls basketball coach was in every sense a spiritual experience, as much as if it were a higher, bigger calling that constantly pulled me and my team toward it. Despite the mounting tension as we drove for each title, I felt a peace deep inside my mind and conscience as I believed in my mind and felt in my heart that all things would align perfectly to create in reality the dominant focus we had crafted in our imaginations at the beginning of the season. And working toward that focus with strict discipline and an unwavering belief that people can manifest back into their lives what they believe in their heart, we did.

—*Coach Burt*

Obviously, these rock-star themed initiatives are out-growths from a theme to which people can aspire, which generates discussion, and which stems from an emotional response. But beyond the security of serving as an emotional anchor that can unite the tribe, the dominant focus also provides the basis to know whether the tribe is winning or losing. It's a lot like a scoreboard, which we will discuss in a subsequent section of this chapter.

Tribe members without a focus will jump from one thing to another, seldom (if ever) being productive. While their intentions may be as good as gold, a lack of understanding and/or unity in their efforts (as well as a lack of a common passion) will lead to scattered results at best.

One of Stephen Covey's famous axioms is, "The main thing is to keep the main thing the main thing." The dominant focus is the "main thing"—the spring from which all of the tribe's energies should flow. However, it's possible to allow a certain amount of flexibility for subsets of the tribe. After all, each group/department/division/staff/and so on may have its own role to play in achieving the dominant focus, whether it is a sales goal, building stronger client relationships, reaching a new market, or developing a new skill. As such, each one will likely need to take numerous small, specific-to-them action steps within the context of the dominant focus to create a major movement forward. Of course, each subset must share the dominant focus; otherwise, they'll find themselves operating in an isolated vacuum, producing results related only to their group that aren't tied to the overall tribal focus.

As we've stated previously, the initial step's job is to build a theme that prompts people to emotionally connect with a dominant focus, which will then incite constant conversation. These elements let tribe members concentrate on how to make that focus's dream into a reality. They can align their thoughts and energies to accelerate real progress toward that dream of the bigger, better future they are anxious to create.

Two other important outcomes will also emerge from this: the tribe will develop a personality, and will become laser-focused on the end prize, which will in turn eliminate many unnecessary, unproductive elements of their work.

You may have guessed that a couple of former coaches couldn't write a book without including at least one quote from the late legendary men's college basketball coach John Wooden, nicknamed "The Wizard of Westwood" for winning 10 national championships at UCLA. Among the many powerful quotes from his prolific post-career writings, we found this: "Great Leaders are always out in front with a banner rather than behind with a whip." Undoubtedly, Coach Wooden hit the bull's eye with laser-like accuracy (as usual); yet we can pose three logically extended inquiries upon reading that quote: *But Coach, what should that banner be? How do I go about creating it? And how should I then go about using it to lead?*

You certainly know the answers to the first two questions by now. You also know that someone with the most impeccable leadership credentials relied upon a dominant focus to lead his ultra-successful team.

The challenge lies in the day-to-day activity. By creating a dominant focus, tribe members can decide on what is the highest value of their time. The filter is the dominant focus.

Imagine a real estate team that wants each of their agents to increase the number of homes sold by the amount of the respective ages. So the 38-year-old now knows the mark is to sell 38 more than last year, and the 27-year-old knows that the focus is to sell 27 more than the year before.

At this point, a Z&C Leader would roll out several activities that keep the dominant focus alive and emotionally connected for each team member. They would hold Monday morning meetings focused on lead indicators answering how they are going to attract business in the week. On Wednesdays they would provide one hour of education focused on growing the Model. On Friday, they bring an autopsy of what worked and what did not work. This forces people in the jungle to have a plan of attack of how to kill something and bring it back to the tribe. An emotional component of this would be birthday celebrations at certain milestones celebrating agents' successes sold during a defined time period.

As we move through this chapter, you'll know how to use the dominant focus like that banner Coach Wooden described as we further explain how to set the other elements of the Model into motion.

2.Empower with Excellence

Equation: Good Goals + Right Roles = Lit Coals

If you have lived in modern Western civilization, then you have doubtlessly been immersed in this day and age's volumes of information about goal-setting. Although we've long since passed the state of being goal-oriented and ventured into goal-obsessed, goals are probably one of the most overused-yet-underdone concepts going today. How many times have you or members of your tribe set goals, not achieved them, and then lowered them—only to either miss the newly reset goal and repeat the process fruitlessly, or achieve only mediocre outcomes that don't result in any real change? Have you ever wondered how or why this phenomenon is so commonplace?

The reason is very simple: *randomly set goals rarely work*. And the main reason why is that they don't include the *emotional staying power* that a dominant focus does. Without this kind of passionate attachment, tribe members will often negotiate goals downward based on external variables, their moods, or momentary circumstances—or otherwise find themselves without the emotional fuel necessary to ensure follow-through.

Turning Employees into Rock Stars: Our First Emotional Pull

One of the first emotional pulls we created that utilized the concept of a dominant focus was for FirstBank, Tennessee's largest independently owned bank with over 500 employees in 45 cities throughout the state. This initiative was a creative adaptation of the concept of player/team rewards that incentivized FirstBank associates to become superstars of their industry by opening 10,000 checking accounts in the 2009 calendar year.

(continued)

To do this, we established a theme called Rock Star Management, which we created as a fun-injected platform to which people could directly relate. The program gave incentives to FirstBank employees to become top producers so that they could be recognized among their peers as rock stars.

The concept was simple: to be treated like rock stars, employees had to produce like rock stars, which necessitated movement on two fronts. Not only did they have to create a customer following, they also had to create an *internal* following. However, perhaps the most important element of the program was how we tied the incentive plan to the four parts of a person's nature: body, heart, mind, and spirit.

The results of FirstBank's Rock Star Management program were nothing short of astounding. They opened 10,645 accounts that year, which represented a 43 percent increase over 2008—a truly remarkable number, especially considering that just over 7,000 accounts were opened in 2008! These accounts represented $2.2 million in new revenue for FirstBank. Additionally, account retention increased drastically from 2009 by more than half.

When we saw results like these, we knew we were on the right track. Why was the blueprint successful? It had an emotional pull that helped people come alive!

—*Colby Jubenville*

Although we recognize the dysfunction commonly associated with goals and goal-setting, we still must stress their importance in your tribe's strategic success. We simply encourage you to do them *correctly*, not to do away with them. After a good bit of reading on the topic, we found some fairly uniform agreement about three qualities that good goals should have. Then we added an ultra-important fourth one.

1. Good goals should be **clear.**

   By this, we mean something that is free from obscurity (hard to determine), indistinctiveness (hard to identify), ambiguity (vague or having multiple meanings); is easy to understand; and is uniformly perceived. Hit those marks, and you've induced clarity into the goal-creating mix. For example, I will have three face-to-face meetings this week.

2. Good goals should be **specific.**

   A *specific* goal is one that you can easily identify, characterize, or describe; one that's directly fitted for a certain purpose; easily defined; and that is particular, precise, and sharply exact. For example, I will identify two people I need to connect with in order to grow my influence.

3. Good goals should be **measurable.**

   Measurability can happen in a quite number of ways. Our sources collectively stated that it occurs by assessing dimensions, qualities, quantities, or capacities determined through comparison with certain standards, bases, or rankings. The sources we examined also had another way to phrase it: Any maneuver made as part of progress toward a goal or an ordered reference, which segues nicely into our fourth goal quality. For example, this quarter I will lose 10 pounds!

4. Good goals should be inextricably **linked to the tribe's dominant focus and emotional pull.**

   During the planning process, Z&C Leaders should cultivate only goals that emotionally connect the tribe to its dominant focus. Goals like "to improve 10 percent next year" or "to get rid of the dysfunction of our management team" have little explicit, obvious connection to a dominant focus. They're simply statements of preference that can be loosely interpreted to fit any mental construct or pet peeve. Also, they can easily change meaning depending on someone's mood or another temporary circumstance. And they can completely lack the rationale needed to explain *why* the goals incorporated certain quantities (e.g., why 10 instead of 5 or 50 percent?). For example, if the dominant focus is to become the best service provider in our space, I could reward my team for great acts of service with great books on customer service.

Clear, specific, measurable goals work, because we can break them down into quarterly, monthly, weekly, and daily increments of progress. More important, they are explicitly connected to a dominant focus. This helps both managers and subordinates organize their efforts toward daily activities that concentrate on things like sales processes and customer service activities, which are systematically connected to organizations' dreams. Because they're loaded with an emotional pull, these good goals allow people to do more of the things they want to do and less of the things they feel forced to do, thereby letting the tribe live out its personality.

Succinctly stated, good goals are *thematically connected* to something that people relate to—*not* something cliché' or vague like "*Win in 2010.*" Z&C Leaders enter into the goal-setting process with a mindset that says, "Let's create something that people can visualize and then drive toward by connecting employees, customers, and our organization with specific rewards and incentives." So many organizations fail miserably at this juncture of planning, then wonder why their meetings have no energy, why their culture has no purpose, and why their people have no fire, enthusiasm, or passion.

Well-formed goals also prompt Z&C Leaders to create themes regarding organizational direction that engage employees. They clearly support each individual's role in achieving organizational and individual successes. Such bridges of communication better motivate tribe members, since leaders are celebrating themes that matter to employees. And who doesn't enjoy talking about things for which they have a passion and zeal?

Unique Perspective: Seeing Opportunity and not Challenge

When Colby and I first began working together in early 2007, we devised an idea called *10,000 Feet And Climbing*, really as a way to solve a logistical problem that seemed to not have a solution. After many attempts to book a flight to speak in Miami, Florida, in the morning and Jackson, Mississippi, in the afternoon of the same day, it became increasingly clear that I would not be able to speak at one of the engagements. I didn't like that and knew we could find a way to win.

I called Colby and challenged him to figure out a way to get to both speaking engagements, and we went back and forth for about three hours talking about possible solutions.

During that time, I booked both speaking engagements and let both groups know—*We will be there.*

And here is how we did it. The concept was to create a unique value proposition to both reward and coach people simultaneously while on a private jet. Specifically, we wanted to reach out to top executives by allowing them to be part of two behind-the-scenes-experiences and travel with us to both speaking engagements in Miami and Jackson, via a private jet originating in Nashville.

On the flight that day was Phil Cavender, CEO of Cavender Financial Group; Kendra Cooke, a real estate rock star; Dr. Jamie Grider, one of Murfreesboro's best dentists; Rick Kloete, CEO of a retained search firm; myself, Colby Jubenville, and our crew.

During the flights, we talked exclusively about growth, and the entire excursion was filmed as a teaching/marketing tool. Each person left that experience transformed, and their potential changed, all because they were able to gain new perspective by traveling above their businesses, looking down, and saying, "This is where I want my organization to go"!

By placing them in an environment that aligned them with peers but isolated them from the ringing phones, personnel parades, and endless e-mails, it offered them unlimited potential for discovery by breaking through the figurative and literal ceilings of their worlds. Each participant said s/he gained a greater amount of clarity as a result of that experience because each was inspired in some way to go beyond previously set boundaries. To them, the fee was an investment, not an expense.

—*Coach Burt*

3. Create the Scoreboard

Equation: Categorical Criteria + Smart Bets = Clear Outcomes

Here's a very simple (but powerful) bit of managerial wisdom we've gleaned from our days in coaching: *people play harder when there is a scoreboard*. If you don't believe this, go to something as supposedly civil and recreational as a church league or even children's basketball game, and watch people almost kill each other because two simple outcomes are at stake: a winner will emerge, and a loser will emerge! The same thing holds true in the business world: the score *matters*.

You can build your organizational scoreboard properly using the following five guidelines:

1. Determine **past performances** (What did each person do over the last 12-month cycle?)

2. Identify **market variables** (How much growth is possible for each person to achieve in her/his specific marketplace?)

3. Estimate **future capacity** (How much do you want each person to realistically stretch herself/himself over the next cycle?)

4. Determine **high-value activities** (What things must each person do to achieve her/his future capacity?)

5. Determine **metrics** (How will each person measure, record, and report their progress?)

Each organization will obviously have a number of contingency variables to consider when creating its scoreboard. However, we can provide a few general thinking points for each step.

Past Performances

You can begin to set the scoreboard by determining each tribe member's previous output levels. After all, it's practically impossible to figure out where someone should go is if you don't know where they've been. To determine the scope of their past, we recommend not only analyzing data concerning individual output—but also to analyze both the organization and each individual with the first part of the SWOT Analysis ("SWOT" is an acronym for Strengths, Weaknesses, Opportunities, and Threats).

- **Strengths** (What advantages does the person and/ or organization have?)
- **Weaknesses** (What disadvantages does the person and/or organization have?)

While this might seem awfully simple (and it is), we must caution you that it is far from easy. You absolutely must have a thorough knowledge of the open systems approach to complete this analysis with any degree of completeness or accuracy.

Another enticing trap to avoid when analyzing strengths and weaknesses is allowing these benchmarks of previous and current performances to become anchors that *prevent* future innovations. We can say this with firsthand authority, because as we speak and consult around the country, we ask people if they think they are using their time as well as they possibly could. Typically, they laugh and say, "Of course"! Then we say, "Tell us three specific things you do each day that produce results for you." Many people clam up after we ask that, for a simple reason: they're not winning, and they know it. Furthermore, they know they must change drastically to start winning, yet they'll still say, "I'm doing just fine"!

Unfortunately, it's usually not their fault, but Z&C Leaders need to clearly communicate that once an organization has made The Shift, employees will get the resources they need to be successful. As a result, *everyone* in the tribe must become a winner, and winning in this case means moving beyond prior and current performances to new levels of success. It must become a way of life in the tribe. If certain tribe members are afraid of a scoreboard because of the increased accountability, or because it might make them work harder, that's likely an indicator that they don't belong.

Look at every top performer in any field under the sun, and you'll find they have two things in common: a coach and a scoreboard. Both of those things are in place for one reason: They ensure that those top performers continue to reach new heights in their chosen fields. Members of Z&C Tribes should be held to no less a standard, regardless of past performance. We certainly issue the obligatory warning to temper future expectations with reality regarding each tribe member and marketplace conditions. However, you need to undertake the process of determining past performances to get a baseline of calibration for building the scoreboard. This is the essential place to start this process.

Market Variables

After completing an internal analysis of the organization and its people, you then want to assess the external environment. This will help you determine how to balance the goals between aggressiveness and reality. This strategy is directly tied into the many customer-acquisition strategies we teach; and of course, each organization and environment is unique. Despite this challenge, however, we recommend using the "OT" part of the SWOT analysis.

- **Opportunities** (What external advantages does the environment offer?)
- **Threats** (What external disadvantages does the environment hold?)

Again, these sound deceptively simple, yet they cannot be done well without sound, open systems knowledge.

Future Capacity

Once you've identified past performance benchmarks and current market variables, the roadmap to success should suddenly become much clearer, particularly because Z&C Leaders can begin to determine aggressive-yet-realistic future benchmarks for each tribe member. Honing in on these sweet spots will then permit them to develop primary, secondary, and tertiary strategies to attain them. To drive a dominant focus to fruition, you must decide which direction to take and how quickly to move—something that's known as *capacity*. Your tribe must have prescribed moves and countermeasures for every person involved, because not every initial movement will help the tribe reach capacity.

You've likely noticed that scoreboards at athletic events seem to get progressively fancier at every level of sport, and continually display more information as time progresses. For example, you can quickly discover a myriad of information at any given Major League Baseball (MLB) game—the score, the count, the inning, the batting order, the pitch speed, the pitcher's pitch count, the name of the pitcher warming up in the bullpen, all the out-of-town scores, and much more—almost *too* much.

Organizational scoreboards must also simultaneously track more than one kind of statistic or event. While it's possible to go overboard in scoreboard content, yours should track at least two basic things:

1. **Activities**, or what steps were taken *daily* to produce results (e.g., the number of follow-up phone calls made or potential new clients met).

2. **Results**, or progress toward the dominant aspiration.

You can then decide exactly what will yield the highest value in terms of advancing you incrementally toward the mental picture of the dominant focus. This is where the high-value activity concept enters the equation.

High-Value Activities (HVAs)

We learned about HVAs from small-business guru Mark LeBlanc, author of *Never Be the Same*. LeBlanc taught us that whether we know it or not, we make bets each day with four primary resources: our time, our energy, our money, and our creativity. These bets revolve around customer acquisition in the business world because, ultimately, getting and keeping customers is the name of the game. Identifying exactly what you need to do so, and formulating plans to do them *daily,* is vital to achieving a dedicated drive toward the dominant focus.

Because results are a product of intensive activity, the scoreboard must display daily, weekly, monthly, quarterly, and yearly results. While some may see this as micromanaging, it is necessary in the case of the scoreboard. Daily activity goals will lead to weekly activity goals, which will lead to business, which leads to results. The scoreboard not only tracks this progress; it's also the litmus test to see whether employees and the company are winning or losing with regard to the dominant focus. Perhaps even more important, it helps both Z&C Leaders and tribe members rapidly determine which daily activities matter, and which don't.

Metrics

Once the logistics of the HVAs are in place, it's time to unleash the tribe, turn the scoreboard on, and let it measure the results it has been designed to gauge. But even when you have some solid measurements in place, the real secret lies in how you utilize them.

First, you need to keep the scoreboard visible and make sure that employees clearly understand its purpose. Ascertain that each person, staff, office, and branch's aspirations are spelled out on the scoreboard. You also want to clearly reassure tribe members that they are not competing against one another; instead, remind them that they're competing *against their own potential*. This will spawn positive peer pressure instead of cutthroat competition.

Make the weekly meeting with your tribe about the scoreboard's numbers an event to which people look forward. Instill accountability by having tribe members physically stand before the group and write their number of HVAs for the week and their results. Tribe Leaders can then celebrate this weekly assessment by rewarding top performers, acknowledging the highest achievers, encouraging middle performers, and giving ultimatums to bottom performers.

While that last phrase might seem a bit harsh, here's a bit of realism about people who populate the bottom. If they're consistently there (and they usually are), they're likely a dead weight for the tribe. Many organizations have employees like this; they suck the lifeblood out of the group without adding anything. For whatever reason, they don't buy into the dominant aspiration and instead continually sabotage it, either directly or indirectly. Unfortunately, many companies and Leaders allow these people to stay in their tribes far too long. This zaps energy and casts doubts in committed tribe members' minds when they see these noncompliant people operating by their own sets of rules (and usually getting away with it!). It also destroys any hope of the tribe ever reaching the dominant focus.

The scoreboard concept uncovers the unproductive tribe members from their concrete jungle hiding places.

It makes it clear that *all* tribe members should—and *will*—be required to drive business each day and be accountable for it. Their efforts in this regard are being measured and if they don't produce, the organization has no choice but to find someone else who *will* produce. So if employees value their jobs, they'll produce.

Please understand that we're not advocating releasing the bottom third of your entire tribe after one week of using the scoreboard. We're merely suggesting that you provide that bottom third with some additional coaching over a period of three to six months. If they don't make progress by the end of the designated time period, then they should be dismissed. At this point, the organization has done its part by investing time and energy to better an employee's potential, and it can then hold the individual solely accountable. If an employee hasn't made sufficient progress by that time, they likely never will.

Using the metrics of the scoreboard, Z&C Leaders increase overall performance. (See Figure 5.1.) As such, the tribe moves forward toward its dominant aspiration.

4. Coach 'em Up, or Coach 'em Out

Equation: Personal growth + Leadership = Teamwork

Another driving force behind the Z&C Model is the whole person theory. In essence, this states that a Leader must cultivate the four parts of a person we've mentioned several times now—the body, mind, heart, and spirit—in order to truly develop their latent potential.

TEAM	WEEKLY HVAs	WEEK SALES			MONTH SALES			QTR SALES			YTD SALES			
		SALES GOAL	ACTUAL SALES	%	SALES GOAL	ACTUAL SALES	%	SALES GOAL	ACTUAL SALES	%	SALES GOAL	ACTUAL SALES	%	MILLER | LOUGHRY | BEACH
														DOMINANT ASPIRATION
														SPEAK COACH TRAIN LEAD

Everybody Needs a Coach in Life

Figure 5.1   Scoreboard

Here is our simple interpretation of this philosophy, which provides a perfect formula for coaching up your tribe members:

1. **For the body: pay me fairly.**

    Though some skill sets are inherently and obviously worth more than others, we can assume that people are working where they can maximize the value of their time spent; i.e., if they thought they could make more doing another attainable job, they'd be doing it. An organization can alleviate the distraction, concern, and wonder inside the mind of an individual about whether she or he is indeed maximizing her or his earning potential by paying that person a fair wage.

2. **For the mind: use me creatively.**

    Few people are so cognitively limited that they cannot find ways to at least incrementally improve their jobs' processes and products if they have enough time. Granted, these ways aren't always managerially, strategically, or economically sound; but a single golden brainstorm from someone on an assembly line is sometimes all it takes for an organization to vault itself into the market's limelight. And sometimes the slightest push of encouragement in that direction is the only thing you need to make that happen.

3. **For the heart: treat me kindly.**

Most people have been encouraged by someone in their lives from a very early age to practice this age-old principle. We're here to reinforce that principle to you and remind you that, as a Z&C Leader, you can be simultaneously strong and kind. Remember the wisdom of the proverb that states, "A soft answer turns away wrath, but harsh words stir up anger."

4. **For the spirit: use me in principle-centered ways.**

Though discussions of a person's spirit are commonly (and rightly) attached to religious principles, we'd like to broaden your interpretation of a person's spirit. Think of the spirit as the avenue for leaving an impact and legacy and a vehicle for having impacts that matter (which certainly still fits within the religious paradigm). With that in mind, we think you'll immediately see the broader impact of this element.

Only through addressing these four essential elements of the whole person can Z&C Leaders truly maximize

The Zebras and Cheetahs Model

their tribe members' full potential. Although the capacity for greater things exists within most people, and will allow them to be better today than they were yesterday, that capacity is useless unless successfully tapped. We once heard a comedienne discussing the use of the word *potential* in describing assessment of prospective dating partners who "had potential" in this manner: "The word *potential* means they ain't doin' nothin' now"! Grammar aside, we tend to agree, and while Z&C Leaders are responsible for changing that condition, they must find ways to appeal to the whole person if they expect tribe members to make a permanent shift.

Employees will not give themselves wholeheartedly to a cause in which they don't believe. They might temporarily perform through goodwill and compliance; but that participation won't be based on creative excitement. These employees will doubtless leave the organization after a certain period of time, because highly motivated people who exist in a de-motivated culture will bolt in search of a place that values their contributions.

Z&C Leaders understand that everyone is passionate about something. They also know that if someone is forced to work in an area for which s/he lacks passion, her/his performance will be mediocre at best. Sometimes leadership erroneously attempts to force people into being good at something they dislike. This will never, ever work. Z&C Leaders should ask employees where their deep passions and natural talents lie, then seek to better utilize those assets while creating an enjoyable working atmosphere.

Coaching and Credibility

Did you ever play a sport under a coach who had no idea what s/he was doing? Though (we hope) rare, we've all probably seen or been part of that dysfunctional scenario, which really only had one problem at its core—a lack of credibility. So it goes in the world of business, where too many tribe members are left to wander aimlessly without credible Leaders.

Tribes must address the credibility factor in order for Leaders to successfully coach their employees. Tribe members must trust that their CEO is also the Chief Learning Officer—someone with a foundation of knowledge and effective mechanisms to impart that knowledge in timely, clear, and relevant ways. Nothing kills an initiative's momentum more quickly than tribe members dismissing it as just another passing fad. It simply won't work if employees assume that the CEO is somehow not involved in or knowledgeable of the new vision's day-to-day operations. True leadership can never regain credibility if tribe members perceive that the boss doesn't get it.

Part of the effective communication challenge and, thus, the credibility dilemma, involves the message delivered process. Variables like organization size, geographic restrictions, and structural constraints mean that the CEO can't always be the one to provide individual coaching; work environments typically do not lend themselves to such synergies. S/he must therefore hire and train others who are skilled at doing so, and who can focus on energizing people through quality individual time or small-group sessions. These individuals act as "assistant coaches," and as in productive player/coach relationships, they must cultivate these bonds through deep intimate moments of shared vision and struggle. They cannot be functionally formed without direct mentorship.

We unfortunately don't find this kind of player/coach prototype in many modern organizations. However, Z&C Leaders know they *must* take the necessary time to make deep emotional investments that will lead to individual tribe members' success, up to the point of adopting each person's dream as their own. Of course, this shouldn't be at all difficult to do, because of the shared elements of the tribe's collective passion. However, it will likely require constant concentration, coaching, assessment, and reteaching of the dominant focus, due to the struggles, problems, plateaus, and even disasters that can occur in the concrete jungle. In essence, the dominant focus must consume the Leader's energy; this is the only way to keep it at the top of everyone's mind, even when tribe members grow weary of the journey through the jungle.

Corporate training is a lot like goal-setting, in that it's another typically poisonous paradigm for many organizations. Given the pervasive popularity of sport, we advocate turning the concept of training into coaching. Your employees might look on this a bit more favorably, and here's why: Coaching engages someone in a set of systematic and consistent behaviors that empowers them to do something tomorrow they could not do today. Granted, that's what proper training in the corporate world should do; however, one of the challenges of the corporate world, which differs starkly from the athletic world, is that they administer training randomly and sporadically. It's seldom built into the organization's fabric. The sporting world, on the other hand, makes it an inherent part of the culture that occurs on a regular basis. Adding this kind of pervasive coaching in systematic ways will create an entirely new concept of corporate training.

But there's more to coaching than imparting greater technical skills. Building great tribes combines training on topics such as sales, services, technology, and information with concepts such as personal growth, leadership, teamwork, and culture in a systematic manner over a specified period of time. And of course, it's all done with an explicit destination in mind.

For a clear example, look no further than the extensive, comprehensive training that occurs at online retailer Zappos.com, which grew since its 1999 founding to be the world's largest online shoe store. CEO Tony Hsieh became famous for his stance that "If we get the culture right, then everything else, including the customer service, will fall into place." This mantra is proven by the company's annually published 480-page *Culture Book*. It is distributed to all employees and contains unedited two-to-three-paragraph entries from employees describing the company's culture. Zappos.com is apparently quite proud of this work, because anyone can receive a copy of the book upon request.

Prospective Zappos.com employees must complete two interviews, one that focuses on their professional skills, and one aimed to discover a bit about their personality. Management deems both to be equally important. Except for staff at its fulfillment center, all new hires (even executives) undergo a four-week customer-loyalty training course, which includes at least two weeks of fielding customer calls in the call center. Upon completion, Zappos.com offers new employees $2,000 to quit. This measure is designed to keep only those who are truly motivated to join the tribe. Employees who refuse make a clear public statement of commitment to their new employer (and more than 97 percent turn down the offer).

In addition to equipping their employees with skills and competencies necessary to do their jobs well functionally, this kind of holistic training also screams to employees that Zappos.com deeply values them not just as workers but also as *people*. As such, the organization will help them build their own hopes and dreams daily via a Model of consistent, systematic coaching rather than sporadic, disconnected training (as a footnote, Amazon.com acquired Zappos.com in 2009 for $1.2 billion, $40 million of which was set aside in cash and stock awards for employees).

"Yer Outta Here!"

As we stated in Step 3 of the scoreboard-building process, nonproductive members should be excommunicated from the tribe after a clearly determined period of substandard productivity during corrective coaching. This is what the "out" part of "coach 'em up, or coach 'em out" essentially says. Many leaders understandably struggle with the concept of coaching tribe members out, but not Z&C Leaders. Type and length of relationships, likeability, and similar factors cannot (and should not) override the dominant focus. Good leaders know that allowing such elements to cloud their vision will sabotage the entire tribe, and its members will not play to their maximum potential.

We completely understand leaders' reluctance to move people out; it's seldom viewed initially as a positive process. However, we encourage you to remember this: People are looking for confidence, clarity, and direction about their future, and they seek to be a part of something greater than themselves. Tribe members who don't buy into the dominant focus are either unable or unwilling to do what's asked of them, perhaps both. For whatever reason, if they're not fully on board, they must be removed from the tribe for their own and the tribe's betterment.

Occasionally, however, even fully committed tribe members will hit plateaus or valleys. And removing solid performers obviously isn't the answer to that predicament. Instead, you might need to try a different tactic: one that will recharge the base with the same electricity it once had. We call this "throwing in thunderbolts."

5. Throw in Thunderbolts

**Equation: Recharged Tribe Members +
Removed Complacency = Reenergized Tribe**

When you implement the Z&C Model, increased signs of production usually emerge very quickly. Everyone begins to feel a new sense of energy; most people are excited particularly if they've previously had no direction or have been fighting losing battles. However, as with so many aspects of life, from people to possessions, the infatuation that this newness creates can quickly erode. Even though they may be committed to the dominant focus, many people are simply not accustomed to prolonged periods of producing at higher levels. It can take awhile to get used to increased intensity, scoreboards, and new culture. Because of this lull, good leaders must create either natural or artificial ways to keep the tribe fresh in its desire to drive the dominant focus. We've nicknamed these ways *thunderbolts*.

Thunderbolts are unexpected jolts to the group that do one of two things: renew their energy, or pull them out of complacency. While the notion of a thunderbolt hitting someone may sound somewhat negative, it doesn't have to be. It might come in the form of an unexpected visitor, a high intensity meeting where the group shares their feelings in passionate ways, an unanticipated bonus or incentive from the leader, or any other surprise event that catches the tribe unaware.

Based on our observations, this kind of weariness usually comes along in the sixth or seventh month of the cycle. This is the perfect opportunity for a leader to do something totally unexpected, like inject fun when the tribe is not used to the leader having fun. Some simple ways include:

- A company-wide rally to reintroduce the dominant focus and paint a more vivid picture of where the group is going, which taps into the spirit.

- A new incentive plan that ties all parts of a person's nature together with her/his role in helping the company drive the dominant focus.

- A plan for heavy coaching to help people reach their deepest human potential and constantly reaffirm the group's plans.

- A series of short-term challenges to the tribe for each month and each quarter, with the aim of making the long-term plan viable.

The ideas for thunderbolts are practically endless. You may need to experiment with and vary them a bit; so, in the very spirit of thunderbolts themselves, be innovative with them. A dynamic guest speaker might be one option. Though some people downplay their influence, a speaker with a distinctive, powerful message could be exactly what certain tribe members need to reignite their fire. Another option is for Z&C Leaders to paint credible pictures of the future for tribe members, break goals down into doable chunks, and so on. The exact format is up to you as a Z&C Leader, but the purpose of renewal is the same for all thunderbolt techniques, as is its purpose of preventing the emotional cancer of complacency.

Like a dominant focus, a thunderbolt should have an emotional pull. However, this is not to be confused with a popularity contest. Z&C Leaders can't lead effectively if their desire is to bolster their own popularity. Driving new results sometimes means creating new levels of emotional buy-ins. To do that, they must present new concepts that allow employees to feel, taste, and touch emotions. This is the thunderbolt's function.

The Power of Human Capital

This chapter's purpose has been to help you deeply understand the power of human capital and forge you into the new Z&C breed of leader—a person who seeks to harness that raw talent and kinetic energy. Becoming the new king of the concrete jungle is not easy; if it were, everyone would be doing it. Many battles and gut-check opportunities will emerge over a one-year cycle of driving a dominant focus, providing many opportunities for you to evaluate your tribe members.

Struggles like these will simultaneously bring you closer with the bona-fide winners in your tribe and help you discern who simply doesn't fit. But remember—it's crucial not to mistake a winning tribe member who has temporarily plateaued for a non-producer. Many who are left alone in the concrete jungle will die there, even those who may have faith in the dominant focus. That's where you put on your coach's whistle, get out your dry-erase board, and start diagramming systematic plays to help them win. The strength of your systems will be the x-factor that helps the group survive the brutality of what it takes to win in today's concrete jungle. And as you build and automate those systems, you must always ensure that no one can slip through its cracks. This is why we included the directives in this chapter.

One overriding theme to keep at the forefront of your initiatives is the idea of *daily progress*. Yes, we've hammered that concept time and again in this chapter, but for good reason. We strongly believe that tracking the daily activities toward the dominant focus will be the single vital, necessary practice for keeping the tribe on track, focused, and productive in the long run.

Make no mistake: doing so will require resilience on the part of both the leader and the group. Daily exertion can be invigorating, but it can also be draining. The temptation to let it slide for a day can be almost overwhelming. Because of that, we implore those who would be successful Z&C Leaders to keep their motivational arsenal well stocked and always be ready to inject some extra motivation into the tribe, particularly at later stages of initiative completion. Because let's face it: it's a concrete jungle out there, and you and your tribe *must* know how to respond while being battle-tested.

Make Your Map

1. In the previous chapter we challenged you to define your dominant focus and The Shift that is going to take place within your tribe. This chapter was about making the map in order to plot your course through the concrete jungle. Your course is created through

(continued)

"good goals" or goals that are thematically tied to the dominant focus. Think about some good goals that could be tied to your dominant focus.

2. A scoreboard helps tribe members compete against themselves (not against others in the tribe). Build your scoreboard using the following guidelines:

   - Determine **past performances** (What did each person do over the last 12-month cycle?)
   - Identify **market variables** (How much growth is possible for each person to achieve in her/his specific marketplace?)
   - Estimate **future capacity** (How much do you want each person to realistically stretch herself/himself over the next cycle?)
   - Determine **high-value activities** (What things must each person do to achieve her/his future capacity?)
   - Determine **metrics** (How will each person measure, record, and report their progress?)

3. Only through addressing four essential elements of the whole person can Z&C Leaders truly maximize their tribe members' full potential. Although the capacity for greater things exists within most people, and will allow them to be better today than they were yesterday, that capacity is useless unless successfully tapped. Use the following to determine how to maximize the potential of your tribe.

- What does it mean to pay your tribe fairly?
- How do you use your people creatively?
- How is kindness reinforced in your tribe?
- What principles drive the legacy you want your people to leave?

4. Thunderbolts are unexpected jolts to the group that do one of two things: renew the group's energy, or pull them out of complacency. While the notion of a thunderbolt hitting someone may sound somewhat negative, it doesn't have to be. It might come in the form of an unexpected visitor, a high intensity meeting where the group shares their feelings in passionate ways, an unanticipated bonus or incentive from the leader, or any other surprise event that catches the tribe unaware.

   What are some thunderbolts you could use within your tribe to provide unexpected jolts of energy?

Chapter 6

Battle-Testing Your Tribe

What does it really mean to be *battle-tested?*

Ask a dozen people, and you may get a dozen different answers.

Many people may say, "It's about coming in early and staying late."

Yes, higher levels of success will require extraordinary investments of long periods of labor, but sacrificed time is only one aspect of battle-testing.

Other people may say, "It requires your very best effort." Without question, greatness will never come about without efforts of tremendous quality and scope. However, effort is still also only one aspect of battle-testing.

So what *is* the secret to becoming battle-tested?

Has the Leader Been Battle-Tested First?

We believe that the real secret lies at the nexus of a struggle and a unique perspective. This applies to both the Z&C Leader and the tribe; but it must first and foremost be applicable to the Z&C Leader before it can translate to the tribe.

In other words, *you cannot battle-test others as a Z&C Leader until you have been battle-tested yourself.*

You're Not Ready Until You're Ready

One would think that if someone started coaching sports at 15 years old and did that for the next 15 years, the thought of walking away from it would keep that person up at night. It did for me, but not for the reasons you might assume.

I didn't stay up at night because I was afraid of leaving the game of basketball after a very successful run as a high school girls' basketball coach. I stayed up because I felt I had a bigger future inside me that was being limited by my current situation.

Someone who is deeply, intrinsically motivated can only stay on a team where there is no future growth, no change in the culture, and no opportunity for future advancement, for so long. I was struggling internally as an entrepreneurially minded person stuck in a bureaucratic world.

At the end of every season, I'd go away to collect my thoughts, think about my future, and decide whether I still had a burning desire to do what I'd done for so many years. Did I want to continue to endure 80-hour workweeks, the endless drama that comes with high school sports, and the present lack of appreciation of the challenging work that I and so many others were doing with and for young people that would pay huge dividends for them later in life.

Zebras and Cheetahs

I decided in 2008 that I *didn't* have that desire anymore, and that it was time for a new chapter in my life. To use a Jim Collins analogy, I was simply on the wrong bus. Although we had served each other well for more than a decade, it was no longer a win-win situation. I was ready to move on.

I was excited and on fire for the infinite possibilities that becoming an entrepreneur would offer me. However, I was even more excited about the impact I could have on the world through speaking, coaching, training, and leading people in all walks of life.

I'm several years into the journey now, and I've not been disappointed. I've loved embracing my new role and calling in life. However, had it not been for the battle-testing I endured while coaching, I wouldn't have been able to do what I'm doing now.

The daily coaching grind taught me several valuable things that would serve me well in the business arena: how to optimally place people within a system to maximize their potential; how to blend individuals from various backgrounds into one unified group; how to cultivate a dominant focus and work backward from that dream; and how to vigilantly cultivate a culture that constantly produces successful outcomes.

Coaching gave me a forum to test theories I derived from my discipleship of Covey's work and the whole person theory, and I'm now able to relate them well to

(continued)

(Continued)

businesses around the world. Because I was battle-tested as a high school basketball coach, I knew I had what it took to play at a higher level. *Until you are battle-tested by getting in the game, sharing some struggle, and using adversity as the fuel for something bigger, you'll just stay where you are and complain about the results you're getting.*

—*Coach Burt*

It's not hard to tell whether you, or those around you, qualify as a battle-tested zebra/cheetah. You can make a quick, accurate assessment along two basic criteria, as follows.

1. Have You Successfully Wrestled with and Conquered a Problem?

By now, when we use the word "problem," we're sure you understand that we mean a condition much more severe than the napkin dispenser at McDonald's being empty. But what exactly *do* we mean?

- Have you confronted an obstacle that blocked your path—that is, kept you from going from where you were to where you wanted to be?
- Did this obstacle cause you to question your very core beliefs to the point of clearly reinforcing what

was important to you, thereby allowing you to clearly articulate a dominant focus?

- Did it then create a condition where you could not possibly surrender, because the outcome was so critically important?

- Were you able to find a resolution thanks to your newfound focus and faith?

If you've survived this kind of struggle, you're on track to becoming a battle-tested Z&C Leader—because the scenario mentioned above ties directly to the credibility of the emotional pull found in the Z&C Model. As you recall, this focuses on a person's ability to share an authentic story with others. Once your tribe members have a basic understanding of your perspective, they'll also be able to understand your point of view and your approach. And it doesn't matter whether your perspective has come as a result of past experiences, relationships, or people in your life. The credibility that the story of your struggle (and how you overcame) creates is absolutely essential to fostering the trust required to take the second step in becoming a battle-tested Z&C Leader.

2. Can You Use Your Story to Create a Model of Behavior That Will Entice Others to Engage in the Present Struggle with You?

If your tribe is to become battle-tested, it must celebrate shared struggle. But let's face facts: people will not willingly involve themselves in problematic conditions unless the outcome is absolutely vital to them (hence our previous chapter on the dominant focus). Therefore, you must prove to your tribe that they, too, have some skin in the game. Without it, they'll never become battle-tested.

And people certainly won't make this investment if they don't believe that you are going to do the same. You can prove to others that the struggle has meaning to you in infinite ways; but whatever approach you choose, you have to convince them that you have skin in the game as well. They must not assume that you're resting on the laurels of past Concrete Jungle struggles. It's so simple that it's almost a cliché, but it remains absolutely true. As much as we hear about "leading by example," we seldom hear formulas for *how* to do that. Now you have one: convince your tribe that they need to have skin in the game, and convince them that you do, too!

As you'll see in the accompanying sidebars, we can speak so strongly to the concept of battle-testing because both of us have been through our own individual battles. These struggles have allowed us to absorb enough lessons from them that we're able to pass along the insights to you. We believe that you can learn another strong lesson on becoming battle-tested from an incident we jointly encountered; however, we will wait to share that with you at the end of this chapter.

Has the Tribe Been Battle-Tested, Too?

In a perfect world, we would be able to tell you that paths to success aren't riddled with problems. But since you already know we don't live in a perfect world, we can't tell you that you and your tribe won't face difficulties. We also can't tell you that becoming battle-tested is optional, because it simply isn't—not in today's world!

We're continually amazed as we speak and consult at how often managers admit to us (either directly or indirectly) that they don't know if their subordinates can implement our recommendations, mostly because they are unsure whether these subordinates are qualified to do so. We know immediately, then, that their tribes haven't been battle-tested (and are also well aware that their managers haven't either!). A manager who chooses not to battle-test his or her tribe in a modern organization is akin to a teacher who teaches lessons without testing afterward. In both scenarios, you simply can't tell if your students are equipped to do what they need to do.

What's even worse is that too many managers choose to place their subordinates in the current of the urgent, despite knowing that subordinates have not been adequately battle-tested. This is equivalent to a coach sending players into a game without ever requiring them to practice.

Z&C Leaders realize that they absolutely must battle-test their tribes, which puts the pressure to apply this concept to their people squarely on them. They also understand that while they can enhance leadership through others' experience and insights, they cannot outsource it. They are therefore ultimately responsible for the tribe's success or failure (a scenario commonly known as the omnipotent viewpoint of management).

If you've stayed with us to this point, we will assume you've given us the benefit of the doubt and at least moderately agree that you must battle-test tribes to facilitate organizational success. You're probably wondering, however, exactly *how to* create circumstances that will complete this battle-testing. Because all organizations and their environments differ, we can't write you an exact prescription on how to make that happen. But we can provide a couple of thinking points that will allow you to initiate the planning process.

Before battle-testing begins, though, and before you put those thinking points into motion, you must develop an intimate knowledge of your tribe's makeup to optimize the process.

A Letter from a Warrior to a Z&C Leader

I was battle-tested by my college football coach, Tommy Ranager. It was his belief that if you could survive him, you could survive anything. He passed away in 2010, and if I could write a letter to him, here is what I would say:

> You were definitely old style blood and guts. We knew that little smile you'd wear when one of us was challenged came from your own similar experiences. You knew what lay ahead for us, and you were preparing us for that. You could trust in us when we faced adversity because you had already battle-tested every one of us.
>
> I've come to realize that you could do that because you made it through some tough times yourself, and had to prove yourself every step of the way.

I have also realized that what you taught us is almost completely lost in today's world. People face obstacles nowadays not knowing if they can conquer them. But we knew we could because of the pure belief you bred within us. This belief came from the success we enjoyed by surviving the "practices" you put us through each day. And when we were against the wall and looked into the eyes of those around us, we knew we couldn't possibly let each other down.

Since then, other people have ask me to explain it; but I tell them that it's impossible to understand until you know for sure that the guy next to you would absolutely come through for you. This is the only way to truly understand what being battle-tested really means. That is what you stood for: Be a warrior, step up, and when it's all over, you have gained respect, no matter the outcome.

Our enduring ability to conquer is a testament to you and your legacy. That kind of toughness cannot be bought—only earned.

—*Colby Jubenville*

The Makeup of Your Tribe

While the specific job roles of tribe members will obviously differ, you can generally characterize most according to their collective psychological traits. We've based these types on the hundreds of people in the organizations in which we've worked and with which we've consulted. We've also added some strategies for managing them. Consider your own tribe as you read these, and whether you can start to put names and faces together.

Runts: These are new tribal members who must undergo an onboarding process that will allow them to better understand the tribe, its dominant aspiration, and the Z&C Model. And this onboarding process does *not* include showing them where the copier is located, or helping them set up an e-mail account. You need to clearly and directly work with these new tribe members by explaining to them exactly what the next 90 days will be like for them, the top three challenges they will face, and where, or from whom, they can obtain the resources they'll need to solve those challenges.

Gatherers: These tribe members spend their time picking up pieces (sometimes related, sometimes not) left by abandoned, wrecked, or misfit work initiatives. They constantly ask, "What am I supposed to do with all of this?" or "How am I supposed to fix this?" These people should receive mentorship from a warrior or elder depending on the role they play. Gatherers will often say things like, "I am not comfortable with _____," which is code for, "I really don't want to do what you are asking me to do." Senior tribe members have to work with gatherers to help them understand or reinforce the organization's big-picture vision. They can help to clarify how gatherers can aim their specific work toward helping this vision become a reality.

Hunters: These are aggressive, focused tribal members who enjoy being in the field. They understand that their assignment is to find the food source and drag it home so that the tribe benefits in some way. These people play a critical role as the lifeblood of the tribe. The tribe does not exist without them, because they bring in business deals, customers, revenue, or other inputs into the system that sustain it. However, because they spend so much time afield—that is, they are completely or semi-detached from the rest of the organization's members while performing their duties—they may do things that fall outside of the tribe's dominant aspiration. This can create confusion and resentment among other members. They may also not be so keen on details or other elements of fulfillment and execution; after all, as they'll tell you, they're only responsible for obtaining the food, not prepping, cooking, or serving it. They don't understand the concept that it's easier to keep customers than get new ones. They want to get new ones and let someone else take it from there. The key to successfully managing hunters is to position them so that they are hunting what the tribe needs to be killing, in order to align them well with the tribe's big-picture focus and dominant aspiration. Burden them with as little back-end systematic throughput and output processes as possible.

Warriors: The warriors are easily identified. They stand out among their peers, speak the tribe's language, connect that language accurately to others, and use it as a way to recruit and attract the right people and opportunities. More importantly, they fight the tribe's battles;

Battle-Testing Your Tribe

that is, they seize the opportunities they see in the environment and thwart the threats by utilizing the tribe's strengths and diminish its weaknesses. They also act as the tribe's problem-solvers and don't mind getting their hands dirty with the details of resolving a gritty situation.

Elders: Admittedly, we live in a world where young tribal members have several distinct advantages. Their exposure to highly advanced technology; broad, deep, and early contact to many facets of life; and a high standard of living have all conspired to create an indomitable spirit inside a highly capable breed of tribal members. We can witness their far-reaching influence throughout modern culture and through plenty of examples.

At age 36, Mike Tomlin coached the Pittsburgh Steelers to a Super Bowl victory in 2009, becoming the youngest head coach to win the National Football League's crown. Jeff Bezos founded Amazon.com at age 30. Blake McCoskie founded Toms Shoes at age 29. The late Steve Jobs was worth more than $100 million by age 25 after starting Apple at age 24. At age 20, NASCAR driver Trevor Bayne won the Daytona 500, the Super Bowl of NASCAR races.

While young people continue to expand their capacities, shape culture, and broaden horizons for all of us, one resource that often goes untapped in most tribes is the wisdom found in those who've been its longest-standing members. Admittedly, some may be adamantly stuck in the past and have less-than-progressive attitudes. But many more can offer unique battle-tested perspectives that even the most broad-reaching young gatherer and or fiercest, well-equipped young warrior cannot. Elders have observed the tribe's life cycles; they can provide insight into future trends because they are familiar with an ancient magical art that younger generations too often fail to practice: *history*. You've doubtlessly heard the cliché that he who fails to learn history is doomed to repeat it. Tap into the wisdom that a good historical perspective can provide by availing your tribe to the elders within it.

Understanding that the tribe and the jungle go through cycles arms you with the focus of your relationship with elders. Ask them to describe the cycles they have witnessed and the opportunities and challenges that were born out of those cycles.

Compare those to the opportunities and challenges you currently face and you should see some similarities.

Ways to Battle-Test Your Tribe

Now that you know the basic types of tribal members you'll be prepping, we can examine the ways you can proceed to battle-test them. There are essentially two that exist. You can:

1. Throw your tribe to the concrete jungle.
2. Create a culture that allows for a progression of battle-testing resulting in a tribe of warriors.

We think the choice is much too obvious to even mention; so since we know you selected choice 2, let's go forward with helping you plan your tribe's progression.

1. Keep It "R.E.A.L."

Believe it or not, many people experience incredible difficulty in confronting the reality of their circumstances. But if there's one thing we all learn sooner or later, it's that ignoring problems will not make them go away; nor will it diminish them. Therefore, the Z&C Leader's first focus in prepping the tribe for battle-testing is to make sure the tribe can keep it R.E.A.L.:

Recognize the adversity: Z&C Leaders understand that *adversity* essentially means, "an unwanted outcome." However, some tribal members can become so lost in the depths of the concrete jungle that they cannot determine anything more than a general state of disarray, rather than a specific form of adversity. Accordingly, Z&C Leaders use a simple three-question rubric to help tribal members see their difficultly more clearly.

1. What are this situation's **exact circumstances**?

   Pinpoint the problems that exist as specifically as you can. That may be as simple as offering piece of advice; however, we know that doing so accurately and thoroughly can be anything but easy. People cannot overcome their fears until they first identify them.

2. How did **I contribute** to the adversity?

   Z&C Leaders understand that *we create* 90 percent of the adversity we face in life, either by our inability to act, or by acting in a way that created the adversity. Getting tribal members to admit this may be extraordinarily difficult, but it's also absolutely necessary.

3. What can this situation **teach me?**

As we've mentioned in a previous chapter, becoming humble isn't some obtrusive form of (often false) modesty; rather, it's a state of being well grounded, moldable, and teachable. Once tribal members acknowledge the role they played in their own demise, they are suddenly ready to be active participants in their own rescue, and are thus ready to further assess the situation as students.

Educate: When tribe members lack the knowledge they need to be successful, you as their Leader must find ways to provide them with information that they can use to assess and diagnose the situation(s) they face. Education provides an assurance and mental stability in the midst of adversity, and helps tribal members find their way forward. Once they become more stable, then they can get busy and move on to the next step.

Act in New Ways: As we've stated previously, what got you *here* won't get you *there*. Part of battle-testing tribal members involves rewiring them to create new mindsets and mentalities. After all, current approaches are probably not working if conditions are adverse, which indicates that tribe members need new directions to take. They can only harness adversity to accelerate growth if the tribe modifies its actions. Perhaps even more important to point out is that tribal members must also cultivate the *courage* to act. We challenge you to identify at least one thing that you fear and tackle it on a weekly basis. See if your fears suddenly start to diminish into resolvable problems.

Look forward to the future: Z&C Leaders must train their tribal members to imagine a positive future while confronting current difficult circumstances, no matter how gloomy they may be. For better or worse, people create a self-fulfilling prophecy that they then live out. This perspective must be a positive one for success to occur. Therefore, Z&C Leaders should frequently talk about and reinforce the positive elements the future will hold for the tribe. Understand that "no" means "no" only for today—not forever!

2. Teach Discipline

We're willing to bet that the gears in your head switched into a negative mode when you saw the word "discipline." So let's shift you back into a positive frame of mind by giving you a more accurate perspective on this word.

Discipline is a derivative of the word "disciple," which means one who has given himself/herself to a person or cause in which s/he believes whole-heartedly. Unfortunately, instead of perceiving this term in light of its true roots, we incorrectly associate it with some form of punishment or forced behavior. As a result, we dismiss it as a destructive element that our tribes don't need, when in reality nothing could be further from the truth.

Here's where discipline comes into play in the concrete jungle: Z&C Leaders must realize that the only functional (not to mention lasting) form of discipline today is *self-discipline*, in which a person becomes a disciple of his or her own cause and future. Anything else really does equate to something forced; and this will only work short-term, if at all. Accordingly, Leaders must do everything possible to create a buy-in to the tribe's dominant focus before they can expect members to tackle circumstances that will battle-test them. After all, progress requires sacrifice, and if people don't see how making these sacrifices is necessary to achieving the dominant focus, tribe members will fail to act and the tribe will remain stagnant.

The Patience and Values of a Saint

Saint Paul's School in Mobile, Alabama, was, is, and will always be a special place to me. It's where I found my voice and learned to help others find theirs. It was more than a school: it was a learning community steeped in tradition. Tradition at Saint Paul's took on a different nature than at other places to which I've since been connected. There, it meant that even mediocre people who were placed into the system could get better by leaning on the greatness of those around you, and of those who had come before you. The St. Paul's legacy was further fostered by the three

(continued)

185

Battle-Testing Your Tribe

core values emblazoned on a sign inside the front door: "Character, Integrity, Respect."

My only problem was that I wasn't ready to hear the message (from second grade through high school), so I probably didn't absorb as much as I should have. Fortunately, I met teachers there who modeled behaviors for me. These behaviors impressed me enough to later help me develop my own teaching style and become a student of the process. I spent countless hours with coaches of various St. Paul's Saints sports squads, who challenged me every day to see myself becoming better than I currently was. These coaches and teachers had the single greatest impact on me because (despite my varying levels of interest on any given day) they decided to invest their time and energy in me so that I, too, could become part of the legacy that defined the St. Paul's culture.

I learned about tradition while under these coaches' and teachers' tutelage; but more importantly, I learned about winning and losing, which ultimately helped me appreciate what it means to be battle-tested. As inherent parts of the games, I had to learn that both winning and losing could teach me something. I quickly discovered that the lessons learned from losing were often much more difficult to discover and painful than those from winning. However, I later determined that these were also probably the more valuable ones.

—*Colby Jubenville*

We may not have completely eradicated all the negative connotations of the word *discipline* from your mind, and you may not be able to do the same among your tribe. Therefore, we have another phrase you can use instead: *intentional manifestation*. Explain it to your tribe in this fashion: They can *mentally manifest* what they seek to achieve by envisioning a highly desired outcome, and then mapping out the steps to get there. Keeping one eye on the outcome and one eye on what must be *done now* to bring themselves and the tribe closer to it will allow them to immediately distinguish between the crucial and the insignificant. More important, it will give them the courage to act in ways that will embrace the important and ignore the unimportant, thereby prompting them to take intentional steps toward the tribe's dominant focus.

3. Create Opportunities for Mini-Victories

Though humble, many Z&C Leaders have sufficient self-confidence to realize that they can achieve success, even under adverse conditions (i.e., they've been battle-tested). However, they must also realize that many of their tribe members may not possess this level of self-confidence— at least enough to venture into the concrete jungle independently, and patiently endure its travails long enough to experience success.

Accordingly, Z&C Leaders must devise systematic ways to herd tribal members toward small increments of success that gradually become bigger and bigger until they experience a breakthrough in greater self-assurance. Please note that this does *not* mean taking the all-too-common approach of throwing the tribal members into the concrete jungle, and watching them fail until they find just a little success on their own. That may never happen for reasons we made clear above, and the only result will be that the concrete jungle claims another victim.

Our suggested approach is based on our experiences as sports coaches. We didn't start our strategy fulfillment with full-blown plays in the first practices. Instead, we taught certain small, simple, separate movements and drilled our players on them repeatedly until they became nearly instinctive. Once they mastered these simple movements, we combined them to create *techniques*, or a series of movements related to the specific roles of the players according to their positions. At that point, we could unite players' techniques into full-blown plays and then into strategies, which would help us execute our game plans.

Similarly, an intentional, progressive series of successful steps allows each tribe member to experience private victories before they experience public victories. This builds a series of mini-wins that spurs incremental growth and fosters confidence. Better still, this growth can be systematically tied to the tribe and its values. This approach will greatly lessen the potential margin of error and negative consequences brought about by not being intentional about the success you desire.

I worked with Christer Czajkowski, Director of Leadership Development and Sales Training for Boston Scientific Neuromodulation, wrap meaning around his training and development process. He had a very simple four-stage approach to battle-testing his people.

1. Teach
2. Train
3. Test
4. Test Under Pressure

Through his years of developing people, Christer realized that testing under pressure was critical in developing their potential. Those that handled the pressure were the ones that continued to produce time and time again for the company.

—*Colby Jubenville*

How Do We Know? We've Been There, Too!

The good folks at USAble Life insurance invited us to speak at their annual retreat in Heber Springs, Arkansas. The meeting was being held at the paradisial Red Apple Inn & Country Club, so we were planning to make an experience for them and for ourselves, too. After all, what better place than the cool, late-winter peace, quiet, and inspiration of the Ozarks to reflect and develop new material and recharge ourselves for a day or two after an easy seven-hour drive from middle Tennessee to north central Arkansas?

Because Coach Burt believes in ensuring prompt delivery of services, we left Murfreesboro two days before we were scheduled to speak. This turned out to be a stroke of serendipity, because Mother Nature had plans for us that didn't involve a smooth ride. We had no idea that we were about to embark upon a 17-hour odyssey through a record-breaking deep-freeze winter storm that would test the very core of the battle-testing message we deliver in this chapter.

The first day of the trip began at 10 A.M. and ended at 6 P.M., when the ice and snow kept our all-wheel-drive Chevy Traverse from moving one more mile. After eight hours of driving, we had barely crossed into Arkansas, a journey that would have taken only a little more than four hours in normal weather.

Since we'd budgeted extra travel time, we decided to err on the side of caution and seek shelter at a Holiday Inn for the night. We were up at 4 A.M. the next morning, hoping to get on the road before others who were planning to brave the elements as well. But as we approached Interstate 40 to continue our journey, we quickly determined that the weather conditions were even worse than the day before. Jackknifed 18-wheelers littered the roadside, and the Arkansas state police had closed down the section of the interstate that we intended to enter. Our razor-sharp instincts told us that we needed to regroup and reevaluate our options.

Zebras and Cheetahs

During our roadside deliberations, we kept questioning what the safe and practical choice would be; but the question that ultimately decided the matter for us was this: "How can we talk about becoming battle-tested if we call and cancel"?

So we battled on. About an hour later, we were able to get on the interstate and travel 40 miles in five hours. At that point, we needed to exit I-40 to get to Heber Springs, which required us to reevaluate our approach one more time. That meant we needed good information to make our decision, which we realized was an important element of succeeding amid being battle-tested.

Battle-Testing Means Finding the Right Information

After multiple phone calls to the USAble leadership team, we initially decided we could not possibly go any further. Then we got smart: We identified a tribe that would have the information necessary for locating alternative routes to Heber Springs—truckers! We were able to find several truckers with positive energy at two truck stops —those who were looking to find a breakthrough. A couple of them informed us that I-40 West was drivable and would take us to Little Rock. Though this was out of the way of our intended route, it would still help us make progress toward our destination. Armed with the information we needed, we were ready to move forward. However, had it not been for a battle cry we had created earlier in the day, we may not have made the decision to drive on.

Battle-Testing Means Creating a Battle Cry

We had been fans of the Zac Brown Band for some time before this odyssey, but their song "Stuck in Colder Weather" concretized for us as we crept down the frozen roadways. We listened to this song more than 40 times on the trip, but after a few normal renditions, we slightly altered the lyrics and eventually began to scream, "We are *no longer* stuck in colder weather!" This became a battle cry for us as we pushed forward, because it gave us a salient reminder of our dominant focus: to get to Heber Springs! Armed with the correct information and spurred by a battle cry, we were in a position to do what Z&C elder Joe Calloway calls "making a gut-level decision to Go"!

Battle-Testing Means Making a Gut-Level Decision to Go!

You have doubtless heard people talk about "making things happen." Many of us dream about things we'd like to see happen. Several of us have made false starts toward making things happen. But none of this talking, dreaming, or pretending equates to *going*!

You will have opportunities in your life to make the same kind of gut-level decision that we did after we walked out of the second truck stop. We drew a line in the ice and said, "It's time to *go*"! So we called the leadership team at USAble to let them know that we would push forward. They were ecstatic.

Battle-Testing Means Delivering On the Promise

After a two-day journey, we arrived in Heber Springs to a hero's welcome. The USAble folks were jubilant and excited to see a fresh face, since most of the other speakers did not brave the elements and find their way to the Red Apple Inn that day. Being battle-tested allowed us to deliver on the promise, a premise we constantly discuss with our clients. The credibility it fostered created a strong connection with the USAble people. And since we fought through the adversity others hadn't, we were able to share and serve in greater depth than we otherwise could have done. That put us in the enviable, unique position to leave more than a temporary impression upon them; instead, we were able to leave a legacy.

Battle-Testing Means Leaving a Legacy

At the conclusion of the retreat, scores of USAble employees purchased materials from Coach Burt and asked him to sign their books as they reflected on the shared struggle and their time together. One member of the USAble tribe remarked, "This was *supposed* to happen! You guys were supposed to be here and finish this thing the way you did!"

Without question, the group left transformed and ready to take on the next challenge they would face, which for all of us at that moment involved getting home safely. Nevertheless, because we had been successfully battle-tested and had been in a position to share it, everyone believed it could be done, and so it was.

Legacy—What Every Z&C Leader Desires

Z&C Leaders build their tribe to stand the test of time and use the following four principles when doing so.

- Legacy Principle 1—The people you hire are the starting point for your values. No values, no starting point. No starting point, no legacy.

- Legacy Principle 2—How your people are coached will define the potential that is realized. We are in a coaching revolution where there is a shift in mindset acknowledging you either are a coach, have a coach, or don't want to be coached. No coaching, no legacy.

- Legacy Principle 3—The systems (sales, leadership) and traditions (marketing) that are created become the catalyst for legacy. These systems become your competitive advantage.

- Legacy Principle 4—Understanding that you have to be better tomorrow than you are today is what allows you to stay competitive. No embrace of change, no legacy.

Along with these principles Z&C Leaders infuse legacy through their people using the legacy sales system.

Legacy Selling System

Great tribes view selling as more than just building relationships—it's creating a sales legacy. Like great coaches, Z&C Leaders teach their people to create a legacy by impacting the people they come in contact with. Great sales people do the same thing through the relationships they build and the value they add.

This system is designed to create feeder systems that feed life into the concrete jungle and attract the right people and opportunities to your tribe. When tribes fail, the failure is directly tied to its customer acquisition systems. They're not congruent with the dominant focus of the tribe and, most likely, not being tracked or measured. It's a free-for-all where good sales people generate new business and others struggle with no plan, no purpose, no differential advantage, and no clue how to attract new clients.

While many are taught to make 100 calls per week, take a certain number of face-to-face visits, and network like crazy, this plan rarely works, which places the company behind in sales in both lead indicators (strategies to get business) and lag indicators (measurement tools to identify what is working and what has been sold). Sales is not about chasing, it's about attracting, but to attract others our organizations must become attractive to the market in a unique way. We must possess more so we can give away more. We must be in the transformation business, taking low value energy and converting it to high value energy. We must solve bigger problems for more people.

This is where the legacy selling system creates impact. Selling is more than just building relationships; it is creating a sales legacy. It's not about chasing but rather about attracting the right relationships and people into your life by making your people and organization more attractive. It's about deep value you create with money always echoing the value. It's about circulating with purpose, with lead indicators each week and measuring the lag indicators at the end of the week. It's about adding value versus subtracting value. It's about taking initiative versus hoping business will come through the door. It's about two funnels that include marketing and personal lead generation.

Z&C Leaders create a legacy by impacting the people they come in contact with. Great salespeople do the same thing by creating impact through the relationships they build and the value they add in a coordinated and systematic manner. They stay in the flow of people's lives on a consistent basis. Great salespeople build feeder systems and these feeder systems represent relationships with super-connectors or multipliers who constantly feed them new business. Other people leverage their time, energy, and influence to send people to you. There is almost always a win for them, but you offer something so valuable that they are inclined to work for you, so it eventually helps them.

The legacy selling system teaches people to circulate with purpose with the right people and offers a concrete plan every week to attract new and qualified leads through the sales funnel.

The connectedness of this system is what makes this approach to selling unique. Beginning with identifying a target 25 and connecting that core group through each of the different sales layers, this system allows for customization of activity to maximize the relationship organizations currently have and those it needs to increase its sales. The target 25 represents 25 deep and meaningful relationships with the "feeders" who are always advocating for you and your work even when you are not present. Compounded with high value activities (HVAs), the legacy sales system will remove any guesswork by intentionally expanding the reach of a sales force. This is not a tracking tool, rather a planning tool that will increase sales. (See Figure 6.1.)

Three tasks a day, 15 tasks a week, 60 tasks a month cultivate toward a dominant focus by creating a legacy that everyone can see. The layers of the system "chunk" people who can help you move your ball down the field into

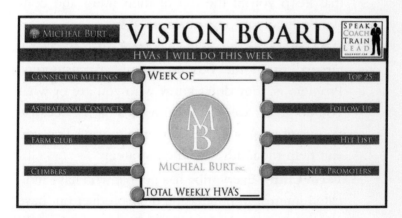

Figure 6.1 Vision Board

various subgroups of influence and legacy. Each week you add value in a number of ways to each of these groups while circulating. Day after day, week after week, and month after month you begin to build deep alliances with others and deeper networks who continually propel you and your services to all new levels of performance. Each of the eight categories of the system is detailed below.

1. **Top 25**—This creates a "feeder system." People in this group have influence and perpetually send people to you by advocating for you in deep and meaningful ways. Your job is to do the same for them. These feeder systems are called "channel accounts" by some people, since these relationships create new channels of business. It begs the question, "What if 25 people sent you three referrals per year that were qualified and right in your wheel house?" Advocates don't send bad referrals. These are deep relationships you cultivate and that keep you at the top of their mind and constantly feed you new business.

2. **Hit List**—Every company has ideal suspects. These targets "fit in the box" of the ideal customers. Problem is, they don't know who you are or what you do. Every week you cultivate a hit list because you want to expose these people to ways that you can help them advance their strategy.

3. **Farm Club**—Every tribe has people who have indicated interest in purchasing their product but have not yet bought their product. These people need

to be cultivated, as in farming. There is an assumption here that we believe: An object at rest will stay at rest unless acted on by an outside factor. That outside factor is you. These people need a nudge, bump, cue, or invite. Once they have a trigger event (an event that changes their objectives in life), then you will be there ready to go.

4. **Connectors**—Connectors have one thing you need—influence. Each week we encourage people to take two connector meetings with people who can connect them to others. These people have large networks, are trusted in the community, and can put you in touch with economic buyers who can purchase your services.

5. **Net Promoters**—According to Fred Reichald (*The Ultimate Question*) there are only three types of customers: passives, promoters, and detractors. You are trying to build promoters who become feeder systems for you. To build promoters you must win people over by adding deep value to their lives in meaningful ways. What is the customer experience like with you, and is it so compelling that people want to send others to experience it? Build four WOWs into the experience from start to finish and you will build more promoters.

6. **Climbers**—The climber is the person who says, "Come back and see me six months from today." They are also the people you identify as future decision makers. They are climbing the ladder

of success and one day will have the capacity of making major decisions, using your services, or connecting you to other key players. Identify them now, get in the boat with them now, and they will help you in the future.

7. **Aspirational contacts**—An aspirational contact is a "mover and shaker" who you can learn from. They have a unique perspective and unique talents and can rev your engine up by spending time with you. This person stretches you and challenges you to go bigger than what you currently are. You should spend time with an aspirational contact once per week and a minimum of four times per month.

8. **Showcase your qualities**—Many times people have great products or services but poor exposure. The showcase is a marketing tool for you to get in front of people in order to share the message and get buy-in to you and what you have to offer. The cycle looks like these five steps:

   1. Get in front of key decision makers or connectors.

   2. Turn them on to you with your outlook and energy.

   3. Make an introduction.

   4. Follow up with a face-to-face meeting or a phone call to assess their needs.

   5. Solve their problems with your products or services. The showcase opens the door. People

must be turned on to you before they are buying what you are selling.

9. **Database, social media, build a following**—The goal of any business is to build a following of people who are buying what you are selling. You cannot monetize a following until you build a following, and the way you build a following is by possessing five important ingredients, including the following:

   a. Great content—Say common things in uncommon ways.

   b. Impeccable delivery—Build an experience that awes people.

   c. Clear position—You can't own a position until you pick a position.

   d. Unbelievable packaging—Don't have a million-dollar brand and inconsistent packaging.

   e. Feeder systems and multiplier relationships— These are super-connectors of people who feed you business and multiply your business.

Each week you share your content through a number of channels that allow your followers to emotionally identify with your work. Your reputation begins to build as the expert in the space and eventually people begin to send you new leads and buy your products.

The legacy selling system uses the above framework to let you pick and choose what your top strategies will be when you circulate with purpose to find which one you prefer. The goal is to marry your best customer-getting strategies with the highest use of your time toward your dominant aspiration.

And that's how you leave a legacy! So what are you waiting for? You now have all the resources to win in the concrete jungle. To make sure you are battle-tested, let's reflect on the one person who battle-tested you more than anyone else.

If you were going to write a letter to that person, what would you say? What moments do others need to know about you that might help you to lead them better? In other words, by virtue of being battle-tested, you now know how to compete on unique perspective, education, experience, and qualities.

You have a new perspective, new mindset, and map.

Now, go lead your tribe!

About the Authors

About Micheal J. Burt

Coach Micheal Burt is a former championship coach, eight-time author, radio host, and visionary. Micheal J. Burt represents the new age leader: the Zebra and the Cheetah. Part coach, part entrepreneur, and all leader, Coach Burt is the go-to guy for entrepreneurs who want to become people of interest, salespeople who want to be superstars, and managers who want to be coaches. He is a former championship coach and the author of eight books. His radio show, *Change Your Life Radio*, can be heard globally on iheart.com (WLAC). Follow Coach Burt at www.coachburt.com.

Connect with Coach in Any of the Following Places:

Website: www.coachburt.com

Facebook: www.facebook.com/maximumsuccess

Twitter: www.twitter.com/michealburt

LinkedIN: www.linkedin.com/in/coachburt

YouTube: www.youtube.com/coachmichealburt

To book Coach Burt to speak to your group, contact us at info@coachburt.com.

Micheal Burt Enterprises, LLC

The Burt Center

720 Cool Springs Blvd.

Franklin, TN 37067

615-225-8380

Also by Coach Micheal Burt

Changing Lives through Coaching

Small Towns, Big Dreams

The Inspirational Leader

This Ain't No Practice Life

The Anatomy of Winning

The Intangibles

Person of Interest

About Colby B. Jubenville, PhD

Throughout his career, Dr. Colby B. Jubenville has been recognized as an innovator and entrepreneur in both academic and industry settings. His body of work includes coaching, consulting, academic appointments, and extensive marketing strategy experience. An expert who helps people and organizations find their voice and unleash their collective passion, Dr. Jubenville possesses a distinct combination of professional experiences that blends coaching, university credentials, and unique insight through his work with industry. His approach to both academic and industry settings helps people and organizations understand how to compete on unique perspective, education, and experience in order to create unique value. His consultation work includes online education platform design and deployment, sales training and development, marketing strategy, positioning, branding, and design and packaging of new products and services. Dr. Jubenville currently holds an appointment as Professor in the Department of Health and Human Performance and is credited for launching the graduate sport management program and leading it to unprecedented success during his tenure. Dr. Jubenville has published over 30 peer reviewed and trade articles in outlets like *Sport Marketing Quarterly, The International Journal of Sport Management, The Journal of Marketing in Higher Education, The Journal of Sport Administration and Supervision, The International Journal of Sport Management and Marketing, The Physical Educator, The Journal of Venue and Event Management,* and *Facility Manager Magazine.* At MTSU, he forged a partnership with LTS Education Systems, Inc. and secured private funding needed to launch the Center for Sport Policy and Research (CSPR) and the Journal of Applied Sport Management (JASM). These ventures have greatly enhanced educational opportunities for students, improved the quality of education at MTSU, brought national attention to the program, and connected theory to practice for sport management practitioners and students. In 2010, Jubenville was selected by the Nashville Business Journal

About the Authors

Forty under 40 in for his dynamic leadership within his profession and in 2012 was selected by Businessleader.com as a Top 50 Entrepreneur in Nashville, TN. In 2013, Jubenville was selected by the Middle Tennessee Better Business Bureau as a judge for the Torch Awards. The Torch Awards are presented to businesses in recognition of their superior commitment to exceptional standards that benefit their consumers, employees, suppliers, shareholders, and surrounding communities.

He is called upon by members of the media for his insight and commentary including; *The Mobile Press Register, The Nashville Tennessean, The Nashville Business Journal, The Daily News Journal, Athletic Business and News Channel 5 (Nashville)*.

Dr. Jubenville is principal and founder of Red Herring Innovation and Design. A native of Mobile, AL., Jubenville holds a B.A. from Millsaps College where he lettered in football and received Outstanding Defensive Lineman during his senior season. He earned a M.S. and Ph.D. from the University of Southern Mississippi. Dr. Jubenville and his wife, Katie, reside in Murfreesboro, TN with two children Jack and Mary Burke. Go to www.redherringinc.com to learn more.

Connect with Colby

Website: www.redherringinc.com

Facebook: www.facebook.com/drjubenville

Twitter: www.twitter.com/drjubenville

LinkedIn: www.linkedin.com/in/drjubenville

To book Colby Jubenville to speak at your next event, e-mail Colby@redherringinc.com.

Colby B. Jubenville, PhD

2821 Cherry Blossom Lane

Murfreesboro, TN 37129